The Revenge Seeker's Handbook

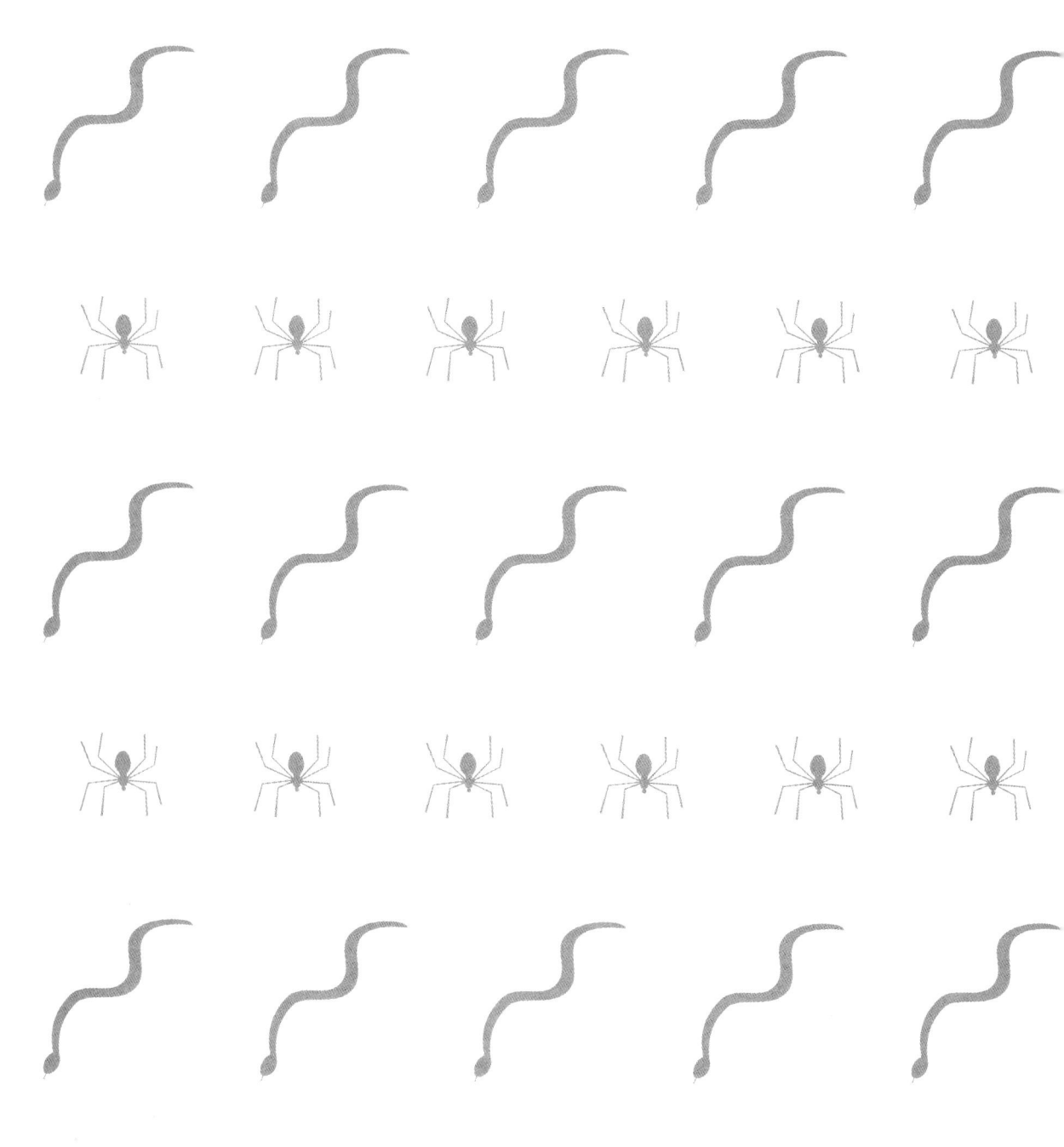

The Revenge Seeker's Handbook

Everything You Need to Know About Getting Even

Adam Russ

ROBSON BOOKS

Produced in 2004 by
PRC Publishing Limited,
The Chrysalis Building
Bramley Road, London W10 6SP

An imprint of **Chrysalis** Books Group

First published in Great Britain in 2004 by
Robson Books
The Chrysalis Building
Bramley Road, London W10 6SP

An imprint of **Chrysalis** Books Group

1 2 3 4 5 6 7 8 9

ISBN: 1 86105 775 X

Printed in Malaysia

Contents

So You Think You Want Revenge?

A Global Vision for a Better World

Everyday, on every part of our planet, people are wronged. People are swindled and cheated, abused and deceived, lied to, ignored, dismissed out of hand, and taken advantage of.

As a race we have made incredible advances in our attempts to bring harmony to the planet and join many nation states that were sworn enemies for centuries into relationships of mutual respect and accord—yet on a smaller scale we are all too often incapable of getting through a single day without constantly engaging in small-scale conflict with our friends, neighbours, children, colleagues, and life companions.

Clearly, what humanity needs now more than anything is a cogent philosophy that transcends all notions of race, religion, and conflicting political systems and instead underlines the fact that we are all brothers and sisters united in the adventure of life on a relatively insignificant planet in a vast and unknown universe. A few simple phrases, a code of conduct, if you like, captured in a book that's printed in every language, and which combines the vision of Martin Luther King and poetry of William Shakespeare with the curiosity of Albert Einstein and the humility of Mahatma Gandhi.

This is not that book.

However, if you are one of the many unnamed and unmourned victims of wrongdoing, and you are determined not to let the perpetrator get away with it this time, then you may just be in the right place to learn how to get your own back.

Victims and Violators

Broadly speaking, we are all either victims or violators. If you fall into the former category, there is every chance that you have been wronged on more than one occasion. Let's face it; they can probably smell the fear coming off you. I mean... have you looked in a mirror lately? Pathetic. If you're crying by this point you might like to order a copy of my helpful pamphlet Self Esteem for the Worthless before proceeding.

If you're still with me—congratulations. You just met the first qualification for being a successful revenger, namely the ability to take abuse on the chin. Get used to it for the life of a revenger is not an easy one. However, for the chosen few of us that decide not to accept the role of victim and instead choose the course of taking revenge quickly discover the many benefits of getting even.

Why Revenge Went out of Fashion

Go back a few centuries and you'll see that revenge was a commonplace part of everyday life. As late as the early twentieth century, dueling was an everyday occurrence across Europe, despite the fact that it had been outlawed since the end of the Napoleonic era. The demise of a recognised apparatus for taking revenge has mirrored the decline in notions of personal honour, along with the decline of other such esteemed traditions as tights for men and public beatings.

The rise of democracy throughout the Western world has been linked symbiotically to the rights of the individual, and central to this has been the notion of personal justice—namely the right of any individual charged with breaking the law of the land to be tried in a recognised court by a jury composed of his peers, and to have access to appropriate legal representation. This all seemed like a good idea at the time. That was before we found out how much they were planning to charge an hour.

Revenge is a totally natural activity, but the legal system has made it one that only the truly rich can afford to indulge in. Doubtless you have sworn revenge many times on those that have wronged you. And almost as likely is the fact that you have not acted upon that vow. The chief reasons for not taking your revenge were probably among the following:

1) You couldn't afford good legal representation.
2) Your enemies had better legal representation than you.
3) You are seeking revenge from those that work in the field of legal representation.

If 1) applies to you, then you just need to make more money. If 2) applies to you then you just need to make even more money. And if 3) applies to you, good luck. Things have got personal and no amount of money can help you now... that is unless you can start earning so much that you can afford to hire your enemies to sue themselves.

For far too long the legal system has taken over the job of a (largely) civilised society that should be self-regulating in the same way that professional sports bodies are. I'm not talking about the big stuff, heinous crimes like murder, armed robbery, or copying the latest Jay-Z album from Napster. I'm talking about the stuff that affects all of us every day—patronising bosses, meddlesome relatives, untidy flatmates, and irritating telemarketers. If for too long you have postponed taking your revenge on these carrion crawlers of your existence then this book can tell you how to make the first steps from passive victim to active revenger.

Revenge on a Budget

For all these reasons, the suggested revenges contained here are ones that anyone can afford. No specialist knowledge or expensive equipment is required. And many of the suggested campaigns are essentially legal. If you wind up in court as a result of following one of the suggestions in this book, please don't hold it up as a defence.

Off the Peg Revenge

Enter the word "revenge" into any search engine and you'll be seconds away from an epic list of mail order companies all too willing to assist you in your attempts to get your own back on your chosen mark (or "target" see Glossary pages 18–19 for revenger seeker terms). A lot of the products on offer can be very useful in the execution of an effective revenge, whether you're aiming for the puerility of stink bomb deployment or, well, the equally puerile but somewhat more involved planting of an inflatable doll in your mark's home or place of work. However, for our purposes, such items are incidental. This guide will make suggestions for the props you use in your campaign, but many of the suggestions will be generic, and it will be down to the revenger to make the final choice on the elements to be used in their own operations. If specific tools are required—and let's face it, the inner child in you knows that there's always got to be room for nauseatingly bad smells in any revenge campaign—the guide will make suggestions as to how you can achieve effective results with things you can find around the house.

Why Tailor-Make Your Revenge?

Think back to Christmas. If you're reading this the day after Christmas, think back to your birthday. If it was your birthday on December 23, give me a break! Which present brought you the most pleasure? The most expensive? The one you'd been dropping heavy hints about for weeks? The obscure one, which if truth be known you're not entirely clear on the purpose of?

No.

The one that pleased you most was the one that you were most surprised by because you were unaware that anyone knew enough about you to choose it. Chances are at the time you opened it you didn't quite know what to say. A common enough response, particularly when you've received bizarrely quilted slipper-socks from your partner's aunt. But the well-chosen present leaves us flummoxed for something to say because we live most of our lives believing that we exist in Sartre-esque isolation, rarely connecting with others on any deep level. The well-chosen gift shows that another human being has taken the trouble to contemplate our existence to the same degree, or sometimes to a greater extent, than we do ourselves. They've taken that knowledge and had sufficient empathy to place themselves into your soul and ask the question: "What does this person need? What would make their life better? And will I be guaranteed pre-Christmas delivery if I order it online?"

A gift bought in those conditions will truly last a lifetime. Long after the wrapping has been cleared away and a succession of material goods has been broken, abandoned outside charity shops, or repackaged and given back to the same aunt—who, let's face it, lost the plot years ago and isn't going to know any better—that well-thumbed paperback, or tatty t-shirt, can still bring us happiness and tranquillity on a deep spiritual level. Because it makes us believe that we are not alone. It stands as a souvenir of a time when our soul truly connected with another's.

The revenger knows this. The revenger understands that in order to truly achieve karmic redress, the revenge must fit the original offence, and impact on the offender in a way that affects them personally. Only that way will the mark find themselves, long after the event, contemplating the impact of what has happened to them.

Like the recipient of a well-chosen gift, the victim of a successful revenge knows that they are not alone. They know that there is at least one other person on the planet who understands just what it is that makes them tick. And they know that that person is dedicated to, and capable of, screwing up their life at every turn. They live their lives in uncertainty and doubt. They can never, truly relax. Or at least not until they have the permission to do so from the revenger.

When this happens, when a tailor-made campaign has your mark at their wit's end, either figuratively, or even literally, on their knees, begging for your forgiveness, then perhaps revenge truly can be sweet.

Self-Assessment Questionnaire

Before we go any further, it's probably wise for us to take a good long hard look at the raw materials we'll be working with. Not everyone has what is required to be a revenger. It takes a special blend of deviousness, patience, single mindedness, and sadism, skills that are rarely valued much these days outside of the dental profession. Answer honestly and no peeking at the ratings until you're done.

1) Your ideal bedtime reading is:
- a) Financial pages of newspaper
- b) Celebrity gossip magazine
- c) John Grisham novel
- d) Instruction manual for Bosch AE6000 Oxyacetylene Blowtorch

If you answered a) award yourself a point. For all I said about these revenges being economical, you never know when you're going to require funds to get yourself out of trouble or out of the country. The correct answer is of course b), for which you should award yourself 3 points. What you can't learn about petty vindictiveness from gossip magazines you'll never be able to learn anywhere else. If you answered c) then deduct a point. Surely by now you would have picked up my attitude to lawyers. And if you answered d) then I'm afraid you score nothing, since the AE6000 has of course been made redundant by the far superior AEX750 range, making it yesterday's news as far as blowtorch-related revenging goes.

2) You would best describe yourself as being:
- a) Outgoing
- b) Concerned for the needs of others
- c) Borderline schizophrenic
- d) Easily irritated by stupid questionnaires

If you answered c) or d), award yourself 3 points. However, bear in mind that you will have to pass yourself as a) and b) in order to be a truly successful revenger.

3) As a child, you used to enjoy:

- a)   Playing in the sandpit with all the other kids
- b)   Going for long bike rides on your own
- c)   Dressing up in your mother's clothes
- d)   Pulling the legs off insects

If you answered c) and are male, then you may want to reconsider your career as a revenger unless you can be 100% sure that there is no way that this information can be used against you. If you answered d) take away a point. Cruelty to animals is neither big nor clever, and there is no place for it in a revenger's code. Unless we're talking about my neighbour's unruly Doberman of course, which deserves to roast on a spit in doggie hell for all eternity. The correct answer is of course b). Award yourself 3 points for recognising that only a few are willing to make the sacrifices involved in the lonely life of a revenger. If you answered a) you score no points, unless you were using your proximity to the other kids as an opportunity to stick gum in their hair, in which case give yourself a point.

4) Your favourite movie is:

- a)   *Gone with the Wind*
- b)   *E.T.—the Extra-Terrestrial*
- c)   *Taxi Driver*
- d)   Any Bette Midler comedy

Award yourself 3 points if your answer was b)—*E.T.* was part of a proposed revenge trilogy, the second chapter of which (*E.T. II—Armed and Dangerous*) was canceled in the light of the surprise success of the first film. Studio executives were nervous about changing the direction of the franchise and decided instead to milk more cash from the series by reissuing the original in a bizarre special edition format where all the FBI agent's guns were digitally changed into walkie-talkies.

5) You tend to start your day with:

    a)   Yoga or a light workout
    b)   Double espresso and a Danish
    c)   Marlboro red and a wake-up shot of Jack Daniels
    d)   Roll-call and cell inspection

Healthy mind and healthy body is a mantra to bear in mind every single day of your life. Failing that, as an accomplished revenger you will have to settle for having a healthy body and a sick mind, so award yourself the full three marks if you chose a). Your body produces all the drugs you need, especially when you're in the midst of a campaign, so cut out the caffeine, sugar, nicotine, and alcohol. And if you're serving a term then something must have gone seriously wrong, so deduct a point for breaking the most important rule of a revenger, namely never to get caught.

6) You were educated:

    a)   To degree level
    b)   To professorship level
    c)   In the school of hard knocks
    d)   But not to the extent that anyone would notice

Award yourself 3 marks if you answered a), b), c), or d). Revenge may have upmarket associations but it really is an activity that anyone can get involved in, regardless of their educational background. And if you're so dumb you managed to come up with an answer that wasn't either a), b), c), or d) then award yourself a mark just for making it this far through a book that doesn't require you to colour it in.

7) Your hobbies include:

a)   Gardening

b)   Watching T.V.

c)   Martial arts

d)   Making abusive phone calls

The major telecom companies all have state of the art call-tracing equipment so lose a point and get with the program if you answered d). And if physical violence plays an active role in your plan, then it clearly lacks the finesse of a worthy revenge. The correct answer is of course a). Three points for everyone who recognised that in order to thrive, revenge campaigns, like gardens, require constant attention and delicate tending. Oh, and a constant supply of the stuff that comes out of a bull's behind.

8) Your star sign is:

a)   An air sign

b)   A water sign

c)   None of my business

d)   Utterly irrelevant

Award yourself 3 points if you answered d). If you answered c) you'll have to lose a point, not to mention that tendency of yours to be needlessly aggressive.

9) Your ideal holiday would involve lots of:

a)   Romantic dinners in five-star restaurants

b)   White water rafting and songs around the campfire

c)   Guatemalan rainforests and hallucinogenic mushrooms

d)   Takeaway food eaten in dingy car parks

The revenger is never truly on holiday. Forget about a), at least until you have vanquished your foes. Embarking on a campaign during b) or c) is likely to get you involved in unpleasantness with inbred murderous rural types or South American secret police and should therefore be avoided. Give yourself 3 points for recognising that d) is likely to be how you will spend a large proportion of your career in revenge.

10) Complete the following statement: "The most important part of a revenger's make-up is his/her…":

a)   Persistence
b)   Patience
c)   Pain threshold
d)   Pants

Award yourself a point for a), b), or c). Award yourself 3 points if you answered d) as you can never underestimate the importance of the right pants. And remember to always pack a clean spare pair too.

Ratings

1–10

Pathetic. You may wish to reconsider your ambitions to be a revenger since you're more likely to be in a far worse position by the time your no doubt ill-conceived plot has come grinding to an inevitably disastrous climax.

11–20

You stand poised on the precipice between mediocrity and greatness. Your true potential currently lies unlocked. All that is required is one last push to send you over the edge. Embrace your destiny or get out of here so that someone truly committed can take your place in class.

21–30

You scare me. Your mind is clearly a twisted labyrinth of bad thoughts and evil inclinations. The level of your mental perversions knows no bounds, and you are only truly happy when others are suffering needlessly as a result of your depraved machinations. You are clearly either ready to embark on your first campaign or for a career working in women's fashion footwear design.

30+

You cheated. Congratulations. You just learnt the most important rule in any revenge campaign, namely that the only limits are the ones that you impose on yourself.

About this Handbook

Someone once said: "Give a man a fish, and he will eat for a day. Teach him how to fish, and he will feed himself forever." Although many a fishing widow would propose a more up-to-date alternative to this maxim: "Teach him how to fish, and he will spend his weekends drinking beer and napping when he could be decorating, helping out with the shopping, or picking up Suzy from ballet class."

In any case, this handbook is designed as a teaching aid rather than an authoritative final word on the subject of how to get revenge in any given situation. Scenarios are grouped under broad chapter headings: Romantic Revenge, Neighbours, Keeping it in the Family, and so on, but there is nothing to stop you from taking the elements of a suggested campaign from one section and applying it elsewhere. For instance, you might like to take a suggested initiative from the Keeping it in the Family section and apply it to your romantic partner. There are no rules or regulations in this game, just sheer audacity, luck, cunningness, hard work, and the desire to get even.

Glossary of Terms

OK, so you've taken the test and feel you have what it takes to be a revenger. Before we proceed with the practical stuff let's nail down a few terms that you'll need to add to your vocabulary before getting down to the main lesson.

Revenger: (That's you, stupid.) Not a word recognised by the Oxford English Dictionary, Microsoft Word, or any editor. But if it's good enough for Thomas Middleton, author of the classic Jacobean slasher The Revenger's Tragedy, then it's certainly good enough for me.

Mark: Your intended target, taken from the term coined by grifters, conmen, and book retailers for the witless saps that invest in their bogus proposals. Note the neutral nature of the label assigned to your victim—emotion is as welcome in a revenge campaign as a fart in an elevator.

Patsy: One to whom guilt is mistakenly assigned. In revenge scenarios the patsy could be your mark, or a third party. If it's you then it's safe to say that you have misread the situation somehow and your scheme has backfired.

Offence: The origin of your vendetta, perpetrated by the mark. The action(s) or incident(s) for which you seek revenge, and which your mark will later learn to regret they ever committed.

Campaign: The entirety of your attempts to gain revenge, from the first crystallization of the idea to the merry wail of the ambulance sirens as your hapless mark is dragged away in a straitjacket for an extended vacation in the electro-therapy spa.

Pitch: The hook that snares your mark. This can be spoken, written, or symbolic, but should be based on your mark's character weaknesses.

Set-up: The donkey work involved in launching and maintaining a successful campaign. Made considerably easier by the prevalence of companies offering itching powder, inflatable sheep, and templates for bogus S.T.D. Infection notification letters online.

Pay-off/Payback: The moment of truth when your campaign reaches its successful climax. Ideally the revenger will be present to savour the expression on their mark's face, though if you're planning on using carnivorous wildlife or tear gas you may want to invest in a good pair of binoculars.

Aftermath: The period immediately following the end of a successful campaign, where unintentional, but pleasing nonetheless, by products of your campaign may be observed, e.g., your mark's eviction/deportation/involuntary gender realignment.

Knowing Your Mark

In The Art of War, Sun Tzu says:
"If you know the enemy and know yourself, you need not fear the result of a hundred battles. If you know yourself but not the enemy, for every victory gained you will also suffer a defeat. If you know neither the enemy nor yourself, you will succumb in every battle." And an anonymous source of wisdom once said: "Hit 'em where it hurts."

An effective revenge should be constructed around not only a sound understanding of your own limitations, but also a sound understanding of your mark. You may think you know your mark, but all too often it is easy to make assumptions. The revenger would be well advised to ensure that before embarking on a campaign that the following information is at their disposal—since much of it will be a lot harder to obtain once the operation has got underway and their mark has begun their own personal descent into a world of paranoid hysteria.

1) Name of Mark

OK, an obvious one to start with, but in the dark days ahead it is important to stay focused on your mark. Otherwise there is every chance that your campaign can lose focus, and an unfocused campaign is a recipe for disaster. Al Gore's push-me-pull-you attempt to get elected president in 2000 is a perfect example of an unfocused campaign, and we all know the disaster that ensued as a result.

2) Address

Where your mark lives. For now at least. Set your sights on having this box read, "Of no fixed abode," one year from today.

3) Telephone/Fax Number

You're going to need these. Phone calls and faxes are central to most effective revenges. If they don't have a phone, buy them one.

4) Mobile Number

4 sndng h8 txts J

5) E-Mail Address

The everyday use of the World Wide Web has changed communica-tion forever, allowing the almost instantaneous transfer of infuriating direct marketing, hardcore pornography, and vindictive hate mail anywhere in the world at the touch of a button.

6) Age

That means their date of birth too. Many revenges work best when the mark is surrounded by their loved ones, so make sure you're in a position to send them some happy returns of your own on their special day.

7) Occupation

If this reads "Mafia Hitman" or "Tax Inspector" you may wish to reconsider the wisdom of embarking on a campaign of any kind. Revenge may be sweet, but there are only two things certain in this life and you would be foolhardy indeed to trade blows with those that deal in either.

8) Marital Status

Get specific and detailed about this—no point trying to break up the marriage if it's miserable to begin with.

9) Hobbies and Interests

Hobbies and interests can play a core part in a revenge campaign. In some cases—building model airplanes, enjoying episodes of Star Trek—the mere publicising of these interests can be revenge in itself.

10) Nature and Impact of Offence

Again, you need to really break this down into specifics. "Annoyed me" will not do here. This may involve you doing some soul-searching of your own. Ask yourself why the offence had the effect on you that it did? And how that might relate to your attitude to life in general? The revenger needs at all times to be both self-aware and sure of themselves. If you take anything other than grim pleasure in the icy blackness of your own soul, take the "Do I have what it takes to be a revenger?" questionnaire again.

11) Working Hours/Typical Weekly Movements

The organised revenger is the happy revenger. Most of us are conditioned to be far too accepting of the behaviour of others. But once you've embarked on your first campaign, it will quickly strike you just how many people whose infractions you'd previously tolerated are in need of a dose of your special attention. Make sure you make a note in your diary of daily progress and you'll stop things from getting on top of you. Colour coding your victims allows you to see at a glance just whose life you are ruining at any given time.

12) Medical Condition

🕱 It is best to check on their general state of health. After all, you don't want to kill anyone, do you? The true revenger knows how to mount and prolong a campaign of such malice that death would be a sweet release, but it shouldn't be the sole aim of the campaign. You want to be smug in your victory, not sorry that it went too far.

Rules of Engagement

At this point it's probably worth setting out a few general rules on how you should conduct your campaign.

1) Biding your Time

🕱 In The Use and Abuse of History, Nietzsche said: "The past has to be forgotten if it is not to become the gravedigger of the present." In other words, revenge, like the Pepperoni Feast Pizza from my local pizza delivery store, is best served cold the morning after. Rush headlong into a revenge campaign and you are asking for trouble. A revenge committed in the heat of passion is likely to be one that is ill thought out, sloppily executed, and unmistakably your work. If you are at all interested in not being identified as the source of your mark's misery—and no true revenger would want to be caught red-handed—then hold off, put some Smokey Robinson on the CD player, bite back the tears, and laugh like a maniac to yourself as you plot your mark's downfall.

Then turn off the Motown and put on some thrash metal. True revengers hate self-pity and the ballads that promote it.

2)   Hanging on the Telephone

You are going to be spending a lot of time on the phone. Just make sure it's not your own. Regardless what you may have gleaned from the movies, it's actually very easy to trace phone calls. And it's not just the cops that do it—all major telecommunications companies take telephone abuse very seriously. And then bill us for doing so. The trusty public telephone is your best friend in any campaign, assuming you can find one that is both working and not multitasking as a vagrant's toilet. Make sure you vary the locations of the booths you use without giving your mark the chance to tie the calls into your own movements. And finally, it's nice to ensure that your mark has a record of your personal number before beginning a vendetta, so make sure you give them a call on it before you commence hostilities, possibly to tell them that you're over their past transgressions and you hope that the two of you can turn over a new leaf.

3)   Spinning a Web

Same deal here. If you don't have a web-based e-mail address, then get one. In fact, get two or three. Sign up with a cool alias that might mean something to your mark, or just a handle that you'll be happy to use in your online campaigns. Keep as little incriminating information as you feel you need to, but keep it all in your secret accounts, and never stay signed into sites. It may feel like a hassle having to type in the name of your first cat followed by your birth date every time you log in somewhere, but if you don't then there's every chance that someone else can get a peek inside your twisted psyche. Abandon any accounts that you feel may have been compromised. And finally don't worry too much if you start receiving vast amounts of junk mail. It doesn't mean your security's been breached and is a common problem for all web-based e-mail sites. Any messages concerning cheap Viagra, remortgaging, penile extensions, or XXX pictures of Britney you don't want you can just forward on to any or all of your current marks.

4) `Pay in Cash`

Apart from the fact that there are still many wholesale and back street vendors who will give you a discount for doing so, there are a whole host of reasons why you should make a point of carrying all revenge based transactions out with the paper stuff that we all thought was a thing of the past. Cash transactions don't have your signature attached to them, and they don't tie you to a place, time, or product. Cash is accepted everywhere and will reduce the amount of time that you have to spend in outlets that you would frankly rather not be caught in, namely Binkie's Sauna and Massage Parlour and J.F. Thomas' Easy-Fit Wig Emporium. Come to think of it, this is a great tip for life in general, whether you're on a revenge campaign or not.

5) The Myth of Fingerprints

The thing to remember about fingerprints is to forget all about them. Unless your campaign is going to involve death, abduction, serious injury, or chocolate donuts, (all of which we don't advocate apart from the chocolate donuts) the police are not going to be interested in it. Don't take this as a slight. One of the hallmarks of a truly great revenge is that it skirts the boundaries of the law without ever quite getting its feet dirty. If you're intensely paranoid you might want to invest in a pair of good quality thin leather gloves to wear when you're writing revenge correspondence to your mark, but even if the police do get involved they'll only have your prints on file if you have a prior conviction (in which case who am I to tell you what you should or shouldn't be doing?).

6) Resist the Temptation to Gloat

Many revengers swear retribution, but never get any further than making a few half-hearted plans. Some even manage to embark on a full-scale campaign that they see through to the finale and then announce themselves as the perpetrator. But only an honoured few make their way into the hallowed halls of the true revenger who maintains a strict code in conducting a campaign—thorough in preparation, ruthless in execution, anonymous in completion. The revenger who spends weeks plotting their chance for payback only to reveal themselves to their mark at the denouement is clearly seeking not revenge, but an ongoing escalation of hostilities.

Revenge should be about closure. If, on completion of your campaign, you find yourself feeling empty or unsatisfied in any way, it probably just means that there is still more work to be done. So, resist the urge to reveal yourself as the architect of your mark's misery, and take yourself back to the drawing board to plan the next installment of their ruin.

7) Knowledge is Power

This is always the case. It may seem a hard lesson to learn, but next time someone is being intensely irritating just suck it all up. This is all material on a potential mark that can be used in your campaign. Remember, there is no such thing as too much information—unless they are describing a hernia operation, that is.

8) Betray no Emotion

Think of your campaign as a poker game. You could try being tricksy, giving your opponent(s) a lot of backchat and trash talk to try and put them off their game. You could even try being totally honest with them and tell them exactly what cards you have in your hand. Either of these stratagems might work in the short term. But generations of poker players have reached the collective conclusion that the less you give away the better. That's not to say you can't express any feelings at all. Half the fun of a protracted revenge campaign against someone who thinks you're still their friend is the opportunity to be your mark's shoulder to cry on. But don't at any stage push it. Real emotions are hard to fake. That's why even Keanu Reeves is on $15 million a picture. And at the other end of the spectrum, don't ever embark on a campaign against a mark that you've told you're going to get back at, unless you subsequently apologise for your outburst and then make a show of patching things up. Remember that knowledge is power, and if you let your mark know how you are feeling then you are surrendering power to them that is rightfully yours.

9)   **Trust No One**

It's a sad fact, but you are going to have to get used to the idea that you and you alone are going to be in a position to admire the artistry of the work you do as a revenger. You cannot share the secrets of your campaigns with anyone. There will always be a part of you that must be kept under lock and key and shown to no one, not to your partner, not to your shrink, and certainly not to your parole officer. A life in revenge is in many ways a lonely life, but a full life never the less, and one that many people are able to combine with having a family, a regular job, and a normal social life. Draw solace from the fact that while none of the plebs around you can truly know the genius that you truly are, if you were to be honest with them they certainly wouldn't be your friends for very much longer.

A Unique Opportunity

And now there remains little to be said, other than welcome to the wonderful world of revenging. Like a latter day guild of thieves, the fellowship of the revenger is a dark and nefarious place, where brothers in arms pass side by side without ever knowing each other and where skills and techniques are passed on from generation to generation by word of mouth and learnt by apprentices after tortuous journeys to arcane Web sites and dipping into books like this.

Take the chance to be the person you always wanted to be. The rebel who tore up the rules, thumbed their nose in the face of authority, and parked in the no-waiting zone. The next time someone crosses you, don't get mad. Get even.

Romantic Revenge

For many years the human race lived in the narrow-minded and some-what smug belief that they alone on the planet mated for life. While the beast of the field, jungle, or ocean rutted indiscriminately with whatev-er crossed its path, human beings alone were thought to have the intelligence and discretion to carefully select and make a commitment to stay with their sexual partners... even if they lacked the willpower or even inclination to always stick to their choices. And so divorce lawyers came into being, but that's another story, and a grisly one at that.

While leagues of paleontologists, zoologists, and other academics have since put us right on the fidelity front with their Disneyesque revelation that swans, seals, spiders, and even some professional sportsmen do indeed mate for life, there are some things that remain a unique feature of the romantic mentality of the human race. Chief among these is the bizarre but commonly encountered state whereby it is possible to be deeply in love with someone and simultaneously wish them to experience nothing but the very worst things in life.

If this describes your current situation and you're reading these words with a broken heart and a lust for vengeance then you have my deepest sympathy—both for the pain you must be feeling and the desperate naivety you must be blessed with to believe that a book you picked up at the last minute in the airport because it had a nice cover might actually provide you with any kind of useful or practical advice about moving your life on. But here follows a selection of possible routes for the lovelorn revenger.

More than any other form of revenge, the romantic strain should be approached with caution and executed with precision. The impulsive revenger is likely to be motivated by hurt feelings, and it's worth remembering that the source of your heartache has a lot of power in the situation and is in a perfect position to turn up the level should he or she feel threatened or encroached. Subtlety and discretion are the keywords.

This is particularly the case where the advanced examples are concerned. In order to achieve maximum impact with your planned revenge, you need admittance to and acceptance in, your former partner's social circle. If not the inner sanctum, then the outer reaches at least. The most devilishly effective revenges will depend on this, and at the very highest levels of the genre will allow you not only the satisfaction of achieving a truly fulfilling outcome, but also one which you have a ringside seat for. This will take patience and nerve. Clearly there is a lot to be said for the short-term fix of destroying expensive items of clothing or boiling household pets, but exes that do this tend to find themselves understandably excluded from Christmas card lists as a result.

With the right attitude, careful planning, and a focus on the long game you may even find yourself not only present for the denouement of your campaign (the unwritten goal of every revenger... or unwritten until now, at least), but also being called upon as a source of comfort for the object of your affections. This can of course lead to the unintentional by product of winning back your ex, which of course the revenger will take merely as an opportunity to eke out further retribution on those that have shunned them. Any revenger who thinks differently—and actually thinks about taking the source of romantic pain back into their hearts and homes—has clearly not taken on board a word of what has been written up until now and may be better off reading another book. I hear Margaret Drabble writes passable romances. For the rest of you, some suggestions for dealing with that someone special who, if we're being honest about it, really didn't appreciate you when you were with them, and probably deserves everything they get.

Let's be Friends

There's nothing worse than getting dumped by someone who maintains that they still want to be friends. But there are certainly ways you can take advantage of this bland statement, which is usually little more than an empty attempt to absolve the dumper of guilt.

1) Taking Them at Their Word

Hey, if that's what they say they want, then be their friend. Continue to phone them at all hours of the day and night to chat about current news events, outstanding bills, the weather. It's important to keep the tone light and breezy, and be understanding if your mark has to cut the call short. Don't be drawn into conversations about the demise of the relationship. Find out the name of their new partner (if they have one) and make sure you use it should they answer the phone. Burrow slowly into their lives, calmly and reasonably, and sooner or later they are likely to snap with the strain of maintaining the friendship they were so insistent on keeping.

2) Face-to-Face Contact

Feel free to drop by. If you prefer face-to-face contact rather than the phone, make frequent visits to drop off mail, toiletries, or abandoned items of clothing. If nothing has been left behind, buy stuff from a charity shop. Your mark may know it's not theirs, but this will only increase their mental torment as they begin to wonder just who the hell that tweed underwear did belong to? Best times for a visit are early mornings and late evenings. This means maximum inconvenience and every chance of meeting your replacement should there be one on the scene.

3) Don't Take Calls

It may be tempting to hear their voice when you see their number flash up on your mobile, but chances are they're just looking to make themselves feel better. Don't allow them the opportunity. When you next speak, say you were doing something suitably fabulous/dismally miserable (movie premiere/speaking to Samaritans), according to your overall game plan.

We Need Time and Space to let our Wounds Heal

The dumper who insists on a total break in contact may at least be afforded a degree of respect for their honesty. However, this will certainly not put them off-limits as a potential mark, particularly if there's any chance that their honesty only extends as far as it needs to for the purposes of their own convenience.

1)   E-mail Sabotage

Give them time to reflect. You need to be quick off the mark with this one, but if they use a web-based e-mail service (and most people have at least one account), change the password. Copy their address book (for your own use later) and then delete it, along with everything else.

2)   Disconnection

Inform the telephone company that they no longer require the service and book an appointment for disconnection on a Friday afternoon.

3)   Message in a Bottle

Send them a brief, tragic note. E-mail or snail mail. Something like "I can't believe this is happening," or "Life holds nothing for me now." Just one line, and leave it unsigned. Now make no further contact, and most importantly make sure that any of your friends who still see your mark agree to say nothing about you, your mental state, or when they last saw you. Even the hardest of hearts will be plagued by worry. Eventually, of course, your mark will discover that the worst they could imagine has not happened, and may even challenge you about your cryptic communiqué.

Deny sending it. This will get them worrying again, either about the level of denial you are living with, or if fidelity is something of an issue for them, who else might have sent it.

There's Someone Else

A phrase that's up there in the top ten of things you never want to hear, nestling somewhere between "Has it always looked like that?", "Where's all that blood coming from?", and "Ladies and Gentlemen, Miss Celine Dion!" It's very upsetting to hear that the person who not so long ago was in desperate need of space is suddenly banged up in the penal hell of a new relationship, but it's also important to remember who your mark is. Naturally, your feelings toward your ex's new partner aren't likely to extend to deep and abiding affection, but there is every chance that a campaign directed at them is likely to increase the bond they have with your ex. A far more effective strategy would enable you to use the new beau as a weapon against your intended victim.

1) Broaden Their Reading Material

A gift subscription is a gift that keeps on giving, particularly when it gets opened by your ex's unsuspecting new partner. Pornography is the obvious choice, though the non-top shelf men's magazines have pushed the boundaries of acceptability back considerably, so it's important to find something that has the potential to shock. Since you're going to have to break one of our cardinal rules and pay by credit card anyway, why not go the extra mile and order something from our European neighbours.

Look for titles with "Hausfrau" and "Schiesse" in the title and you're unlikely to be disappointed, and your ex will have to go to the extra expense and inconvenience of dealing with a subscriptions office in Bremen if he wants to cancel his "gift." But really, pornography is only the tip of the iceberg. Think outside the box on this for real impact. For example, imagine what you would think if you were to discover that your new (childless) boyfriend received Just Seventeen by post each week. Obviously it will usually be harder to find a publication that will shock a new boyfriend, who would no doubt think he'd hit the jackpot were he to find a consignment of hardcore on the mat, but a regular delivery of Brides and Bridalwear magazine should work in most cases.

2)   Call Them

Calling your ex and asking to speak to him when your replacement picks up the phone is likely to annoy both your ex and your replacement, but it will frequently end in tears of the worst variety, namely yours. Far more effective is to get all your mates to phone, adopting a variety of bogus identities if necessary. This will lead to a sense of unrest in the mind of your replacement, particularly if he/she got it together with your ex while the two of you were still going out. Once a cheater, always a cheater, and your replacement has already got first-hand experience of how prepared your ex is to mess around behind their partner's back.

3)   One Last Time

Getting together one last time for old time's sake is a great way of wrecking your ex's new relationship before it's had time to even find its feet. Arrange to meet with your ex at as remote a hotel as you can find and book a room in your name. Getting a man to agree to this will usually be a lot easier than getting a woman to. The average male only has to hear something that plays up to his ego to allow you to hack straight into his brain, and if you're appealing to his groin you can usually bypass the brain altogether. If your ex is female, make sure you use Cosmo terms like "needing closure" and there's still a good chance that you can find a way of getting her to pity you enough to agree to one last session. As long as you don't call it that, of course.

After the act, wait for your mark to go to the bathroom or fall asleep and get to work fast. Get dressed and take everything that your mark has brought with them. Clothes, shoes, money, mobile phone, car keys. The works. Get out of the room, check out and pay, and get out of there. Call your mark's new partner and let them know where he/she is. Your mark won't be going anywhere and will appreciate the time alone you've given them to come up with a credible explanation as to how they got there.

Breaking Up is Hard to Do

Breaking up a relationship can be a terrible thing. At least, it can be when it's happening to you. But if you find out that the light of your life is for any reason no longer worthy of your affections—and you're certain you don't want to give them another chance—then why not have the time of your life ending it in your own special way.

1) Meet Me in St. Louis

You'll need to be incommunicado for a couple of days. This one works best if you and your soon to be ex have a long-distance relationship or are geographically apart for some reason. Phone your mark from a public place— on a mobile or a pay phone, it doesn't matter at this point—and tell them that your parents/boss/fairy godmother has paid for you to go on a trip, and ask for them to join you. It could be St. Louis or St. Tropez, but be realistic with how far they're likely to be prepared to go. Tell them that everything is paid for, the hotel sounds beautiful or whatever it takes to sweeten the deal until they cannot resist and take the bait. Give them details of the hotel— real or made up, it doesn't matter—and tell them that all they have to do is buy a ticket to join you. Tell them that you will reimburse them for the ticket when they arrive, and all they need to do is jump in a taxi and give the driver the name of the hotel as you'll pay for it when they arrive.

Now break all contact. Don't answer the phone to anyone, and if you're using a benefactor in your set-up make sure they don't either in case your mark should get it into their head to check your story. Check your messages every so often, but if you need to bolster your pitch at all, do it by text.

Once they've made it to your chosen destination—and have either wasted a hefty cab bill looking for a hotel that doesn't exist or arrived at the real one to find you're not in it—you can break the news to them that not only will they not be seeing you tonight, they won't be seeing you any other night ever again. This works best on marks that have limited funds and/or a fear of flying.

2)   Hopes Dashed

What is it about your partner that makes you want to finish with them? Is it their unhealthy devotion to their car? Their annoying tendency to always put their friends before you? The amount of time they spend on their Sony Playstation or Nordic Cross-Trainer? Fix on something and send them the e-mail pitch of their lives telling them they have been selected from the customer database to possibly take part in a special event. So, if their crime is to spend every evening drinking with the boys then send them something from the brewery that produces their favourite beer; if they spend their every waking hour in the gym tell them you are from Reebok. The more time you can invest in producing a quality-looking document to send them (by going to Web sites and saving actual company logos to use on your e-mail) the more likely they are to be convinced they are straight off the bat. But if you sense that they are at all uncertain simply stress to them that you are a freelance promotions consultant who works for lots of big companies, and reel off a list of appropriately impressive names. If you can enlist the help of a close friend that you know you can trust (not withstanding that as a revenger you can of course trust no one) that will help with fielding phone calls.

Tell your mark that they are on a shortlist but that it looks extremely likely that they will be chosen to attend the Miller Draft Weekend Festival/Reebok Aerobathon

Extravaganza, but ask them to keep quiet about it until the official announcement has been made. Give them the dates that need to be kept free (and make sure that these dates clash with something that you have already planned to do with your partner). When your mark informs you that there may be a problem with your plans for that weekend go along with them, albeit with a show of disappointment.

A couple of weeks before the proposed event, send an e-mail to your mark telling them that they have been successful and you are going to be in the area and it would be a great chance for the two of you to meet up. Give them the address of a hotel/conference center/restaurant that's nearby (but not too near) and tell them you will meet them in reception.

With your mark away you are free to move your stuff out (or their stuff out) leaving them a note to the effect that since Miller Draft/Reebok running shoes are clearly the most important things in their life, maybe it's time that they moved in together. The finishing touch in this campaign is to drop your mark an apologetic e-mail explaining that the event has been cancelled due to one of the sponsors pulling out at the last minute, but that hopefully it will be happening in six months and they will be contacted nearer the time to see if they are still interested in taking part.

Friendly Fire

One of Us

For many people, friends are the new family. This is hardly a recommendation. If you're anything like me, you spent most of your childhood alternately ignored or prevented from having any fun by your fussing parents and ridiculed or tormented by your siblings. Getting away from home was the greatest thing that ever happened to you, and with the right choice of location—far enough so that the folks can't just drop in but not so far that they'd ever have to stay over, should they choose to surprise you—you've probably managed to knock down the number of occasions you have to spend with them per annum into single figures.

However, just when you thought it was safe to answer the phone again, something happened to your friends. Those people who you were so desperate to spend more time with when you lived with your relatives have now turned out to be every bit as infuriating as your family used to be. Their once-charming idiosyncrasies are now major sources of irritation. What you once saw as a love of partying is now revealing itself to be just another case of borderline alcoholism. That friend of yours with the amazing CD collection has you wishing you could shove their I-Pod somewhere that would make its owner truly appreciate it's rounded tactile edges. And the bad timekeepers have you wishing you could just call a time-out on the whole friendship altogether. Before embarking on a revenge campaign against a member of your social circle, it is important that you fix on what your objective is. Ask yourself the following:

1) What is the scale of your mark's offence?:
Mark them from 1–10. 1, is the most trivial and 10, the most heinous.
We'll assign this the function S.

2) What is the objective of your revenge?:
a)   To utterly humiliate your mark?
Assign this H for humiliation.
b)   To merely correct errant behaviour?
Assign this C for correction.
c)   To critically fracture the friendship in an appropriate way?
Assign this E for excommunication.

3) What is your popularity rating within the group in question?:
Mark them from 1–10. 1 is Osama Bin Laden, 10 is Brad Pitt and Jennifer Aniston at a Swinging Couples' Club Night.
We'll assign this the function R.

4) How would you rate your mark's popularity?:
Mark them from 1–10 on the same scale.
We'll assign this the function M.

Now feed the data into the following model to find the appropriate revenge for the situation: Ideal Revenge = S x R/M applied to the appropriate function H/C/E.

OK, got a figure? No? Of course you don't. I thought I already told you this isn't going to be textbook stuff. But there is a point here. If your aim is to excommunicate your mark from the group, it will be a lot harder to achieve if their popularity rating is higher than your own. This may not be of concern if the rest of the group is as annoying in their own way as your mark is, but it's still worth bearing in mind before embarking on your campaign, particularly if you have any use at all for any of your friends, such as your own birthday or a major wallpaper stripping operation coming up.

1) Phone a Friend

In today's busy society, it's all too easy for your friends to become the people you spend the most time with at the expense of the people you actually most enjoy spending time with. But the rise of the mobile phone means that you never need to be more than a 3 a.m. phone call away from anyone. Just make sure you don't use your own phone.

2) Money Talks

This is a great one for those friends of yours who spend the majority of your evenings out with them chatting on their mobile phone. Ensure that they retain the high sense of self worth that endless chatting on the phone clearly brings them by writing their phone number on every piece of currency that comes into your possession. Add a short message if you like, such as "Call me." They will receive phone calls from anyone and everyone, at all hours of the day and night, but particularly from sad men calling from bars at 2 a.m. who are convinced your mark is the cute checkout girl that was obviously flirting with him in the supermarket some six hours previously.

Pizza to Go

Pity the poor pizza delivery boy/girl. Employed for a miserly hourly rate, sent out wherever basic cooking skills are lacking, day and night in any weather. Liable to miss out on all the major sporting events on TV, with no tip and frequently little appreciation at the end of their journey, and frankly lucky to make it to the end of the night at all if the driving skills of those employed at my local branch are anything to go by.

On top of all that, for years, the pizza delivery operative has had to put up with being the unwitting tool in countless mindless revenges. I'm not saying that there isn't an offence on earth for which ordering a bogus pizza is a suitable revenge (and if someone ate your piece maybe sending them a bogus pizza is just the way to get them back). But let's face it, if they're such a salad dodger in the first place there's every chance that they'll just take the delivery and you'll have done them a favour. Hardly a revenge at all. Not worthy of the name.

That's why today's modern revenger should strive to be different and break with the past. The breadth of service industries available in any Yellow Pages directory is staggering, meaning that your mark is only a phone call away from an unexpected visit from a highly-trained professional who'll be very quickly annoyed by their apparent lack of interest in the service that they are offering. As always, the real watermark of an effective revenge is to let the punishment fit the crime. Some suggestions to get you started:

1)   At Your Service

Get a same sex stripper for the friend who's been flirting with your other half. Or a pool cleaner for the friend who's forever boasting about their amazing (but pool-less) apartment. Maybe a careers consultant for the slacker who hasn't moved from the couch in three years, or a construction/security worker for anyone physically intimidating. An I.T. Consultant for the sap that never returns any of your e-mails. For anyone you truly hate hire a double-glazing salesman.

2) Clear Out the Cobwebs

Apparently, the average Westerner wears 20% of their wardrobe 90% of the time. So why not help out the vainest and most fashion obsessed of your friends with a phone call to help them rationalise their wardrobes. Many charities will now collect if you let them know you have plenty to contribute.

3) Free Advertising

Most cities and towns have a local newspaper with an advertising section in which you can list unwanted items for free. Take the opportunity to list your mark's most treasured possessions, along with their phone number. Or make up an appropriate, or even downright surreal product or service that they might be offering. An unwitting mark I came across once was so bombarded with calls about a garden shed for sale at a bargain price that he began to simply state that it had been sold already just to end the call as promptly as possible. A minor inconvenience perhaps, but after thirty calls an evening his eyes were taking on a mad glaze that even I was beginning to be scared by.

4) Alternative Accommodation

Using the local newspaper again, why not try cutting the cost of your mark's rent by advertising for a roommate on their behalf. Stress that the house is animal, smoker, drum-kit, and alternative lifestyle friendly. Unless they're into animals, cigarettes, thrash metal, or any form of alternative lifestyle, of course—in which case they probably throw awesome parties and you should probably forget about your campaign altogether.

The Art of Revenge Photography

Remember when I said that revenge campaigns didn't require expensive specialist kit? Well, the bad news is that I lied. The good news is that what with everybody going digital these days, the price of a good second-hand SLR camera has dropped through the floor. And so many geeks are out there desperate to get on the digital bandwagon that I'm confident the cost of those babies will be following it down pretty soon. Believe me, that's the way it always goes with technology, and only a total fool would try keeping up with it.

1) Personal Services

A photograph of your mark in tight or revealing clothing, or better still in the suit they were born in, is useful to have for this one. However, the joys of modern digital image manipulation make such an item a luxury that saves you a bit of time rather than an absolute necessity. Once you've got an image of your mark in a suitably provocative pose, add their phone number and a suitably lurid moniker (alliteration

48

traditionally works here, so Helen is prefixed with Horny or Hot, Steve with Stud or Stallion, and so on).

Print as many cards up as you can and stick them up in as many public phone boxes as you can. The telecom companies employ firms and individuals to clean out booths these days, so they won't stay up for very long, but your mark is bound to get some interesting calls in that time. You can also increase the shelf life of your calling cards by displaying them in less obvious places (on college bulletin boards, office staff rooms, and under parked car windscreen wipers, for instance).

2) Can you Guess What it is Yet?

Remember the cryptic photo round on that old TV quiz show Ask the Family? No? Well, good. It was a terrible show and you were obviously either the wrong age to be watching it (it had a very limited target audience, despite the title) or else actually spending time with your family, rather than quietly weeping in front of the electronic babysitter that was your only friend.

For those of us sad enough to remember it though, the cryptic photo was one of the show's few highlights. An extreme close up of an everyday object gradually becomes more recognisable until some bright spark pipes in with what it is. Get your mark involved in a game by sending them photos of your current campaign in unrecognisable detail. For instance, you might like to send them bizarre close-up shots of their toothbrush and the toilet bowl over a week, before revealing that you cleaned the toilet with said implement a week before. This technique can be applied to any number of stunts that would normally be over and done with in an instant, and allow you to prolong your mark's curiosity, and ultimately their misery.

Friends Reunited: Vendettas Reignited

The growth of sites like Friends Reunited has meant that you no longer need to just wonder what all your old friends and flames from the schoolyard are up to. Indeed, it has brought people together across continents and decades, with old classmates corresponding and at least one romance blossoming online into an actual marriage proposal.

The site allows the revenger something altogether different though, namely an opportunity to go into vindictive detail about just what a bigoted thug Shane was in his formative years and how Wendy was getting through a roll of toilet paper a day stuffing her bra before she got married and received the best silicone transplants available as a wedding present from her husband.

Be sure not to sign on as yourself and to avoid the truth where possible. If you find yourself on a site where your mark has yet to register, why not sign in on their behalf and bring your old alumni up to date on your conviction for indecency in a public place and your proposed application for gender realignment?

Fire with Fire

Whoever it was that said "fight fire with fire" had clearly never tried it. And who could blame him for not wanting to try something so patently stupid. Anyway, however ludicrous the suggestion might be in its literal form, we all understand the general idea, and there is certainly no sweeter way of getting revenge on your friends than by hoisting them by their own petard, whatever that means. You'll need to perfect your most innocent "what-me?" look for most of these, but once you've got that down pat, believe me you will have nothing but fun.

1)   Bad Timekeeping

There's nothing quite so irritating as someone who seems to be willfully late whenever you've arranged something (or so my publisher keeps telling me). Personally I've always made it a rule to be so fashionably late I actually end up arriving dorkishly early for a totally different event I'm not even invited to, but there you go, that's just me.

Turn the tables on your tardy friends by making arrangements you have no intention of keeping. Make plans to be doing something else instead and then just don't show up.

Alternatively, arrive on time and then leave straightaway. When your late mate calls to ask where you are, explain that you thought you arrived on time but that when they didn't show you just assumed that you'd got your dates mixed up. Then tell them that you bumped into some other friends and are off to see a movie or just dead beat and going home. Repeat this until they get the message.

2)   Lend a Hand

One of the great things about having friends, as opposed to not having them, is the sharing. The good times, the bad times, the challenges of life, and the observations of those that you spend it with. But draw the line there. Seriously. When it comes to possessions, take the attitude that what's theirs is yours, and what's yours they can keep their goddamn hands off.

If you should have made the dreadful mistake of lending something to a friend and they're being slack about returning it, I'm afraid you're going to have to get involved in a mild form of one of the messiest operations known in human history, that is hostage taking. The history of hostages and ransom demands is littered with tragic tales of loneliness, misery, and decapitation, so you'd best start small; a favourite sweater, a treasured first edition, or maybe their car keys.

If this doesn't work you'll have to think about getting serious and abducting a small pet or their first-born child. Once you've got their attention, make sure you let them sweat for a bit before you start negotiating with them. Don't take their calls for a couple of days, however desperate you are to get your precious stuff back, and you'll be amazed at how willing they will be to accede to your terms. Make sure that you choose a neutral venue for the exchange and that they go first in the handover.

3) I'm Sure I've Got it Somewhere

Some friends are as careful with your stuff as they are with their own. This is OK as long as you're not friendly with slobs and slackers whose only concern is where their next welfare check is coming from and where they put the end of that last doobie. You can give these friends a wake-up call, with a bonus gift handcrafted especially for them.

Take a handful of raw beef mince and secrete it around whatever passes for their living environment. Behind fixtures such as radiators and ovens is good, but if you've got basic needlecraft you could also sew some into their curtain linings, bean-bags, or cushions. The key, as always is to be subtle. A little goes a long way, and you don't want your mark to discover the source of the smells, so spread the flesh liberally everywhere rather than concentrating it in a single place. After a few days, or even twenty-four hours in hot weather, your mark will be returning home to the sweet smell of death every evening and even the most unhygienic of layabouts will be forced to tidy up a bit, and hopefully in the process find whatever it was you were foolish enough to lend them. With your treasured possessions safely returned you could pull on a pair of marigolds and put them out of their misery, or alternatively just sit back and wait for the inspectors to declare their building a public health risk.

Put it in Writing

The growth of e-mail has meant that it's rare for me to come down of a morning and find letters on my doormat, other than the usual selection of eviction notices and restraining orders anyway. For this reason, taking the trouble to send an actual letter to your mark can have a real impact.

1) Doctor Doctor

If there were a chart countdown of revenges then the bogus letter informing the hapless mark that they've contracted a nasty disease would be at number 3, just behind cutting up ties and ineffectively spreading grass seed on the carpet. Go online and you'll be able to find any number of templates for writing the perfect STD letter, but as always, the personal touch is always the best way of letting your mark know just how you feel about them.

And that's going to mean getting an STD test yourself. Yes, you. After all, you're not always entirely fussy after about 1am on a Saturday night. And you've obviously never been told that the condom actually has to come out of your wallet in order to offer any kind of protection. Most hospitals and health centres have drop-in clinics that guarantee complete anonymity, meaning it won't go on your medical record, and they'll give you same day results.

Once you've got the all clear, draft a letter for your mark, using the same format, names and addresses as your own official notification, and pop it in the post to them. Inform your mark that they were cited as a recent sexual partner of someone who has recently tested positive and suggest that it might be a good idea for them to make an appointment.

The test itself is a walk in the park. A quick blood sample and you're out. But what makes the experience harrowing is the excessive amount of counseling every patient is forced to endure, both before they can be given the test and once they are ready to collect their results.

2) Merry Christmas: War is Declared

As a rule I don't get many Christmas cards. Maybe I should send more. Like any, for instance. It all just looks like an awful lot of hard work and smacks of a certain desperation to me. Sending Christmas cards is an empty gesture designed to induce guilt, and if there's one thing you should be striving to avoid as a revenger, it's an empty gesture. Even at Christmas.

Make your own personal statement about the retards that insist on sending you a card every year, despite the fact that you don't even take their phone calls, by getting your seasonal plans underway early this year and sending Christmas cards to an extensive list of people in their name. Make sure you're brutally honest without resorting to mindless profanity. "I've never liked you, but what the hell, it is Christmas" or "It would be really great if your other half could make it to our party without you" are a couple of universal messages you could send to anyone, but as always it's about tailoring it to suit the needs of your individual mark.

Spook Them Out

If none of the revenges you try succeed in getting rid of a truly obnoxious "mate" then the only option you have left is to behave in an even more irritating way than them. Freak them out via any means neccessary or pretend to be in love with them—plague them with phone calls begging to see them or get photos of them enlarged and cover your walls with them. They will soon refuse to have anything to do with you and may even take out a restraining order.

1) Voodoo Queen

For this you'll need a sample of hair from your mark. Take your sample and put it in a jar, the more ornate the better, as the impact of this one depends a lot on the effect you create. Next time your friend does something to annoy you, tell them they will regret it. Resist the temptation to talk about it in great length, but when they force the issue tell them you know black magic and will mess their life up. Show them the jar containing their hair and explain that this is what gives you power over them.

Incidental Revenge

Reverse Karma for Telemarketers

 The people that really annoy us, and are therefore most worthy of receiving a revenge campaign, are generally those closest to us. Friends and family, partners and colleagues, people who we let into the innermost sanctums of our existence only for them to betray that trust by letting slip about our tendency to snore like a choking warthog to potential partners or helping themselves to our secret stash of breakfast cereal. However, in recent years, society has seen the birth of a whole new breed of worker whose job it is to get under your skin and involve himself or herself in your life whether you want them there or not. Ladies and gentlemen, I give you... the telemarketer. Armed with only your name, telephone number, and the scantiest of details on your purchasing habits, the telemarketer has very quickly established himself as the most likely cause of foul and offensive language in the home after discarded Lego bricks and impossible to open milk cartons.

Of course, the telemarketer is merely the evolution of the door-to-door salesman, who these days is as likely to be trying to sell you a path to spiritual enlightenment as a new set of brushes. And so there follow several suggested tactics for practitioners of both of these darkest of the black arts. In both cases you will find it is necessary to cross the line on one of our cardinal rules of revenge, namely to be indiscriminate in your campaigning. Unfortunately it will be nigh on impossible for you to track down the specific individuals involved in ruining the delicate peace of your weekends; staff turnover is understandably high in these foul industries, and corporations are often protective about employees whose jobs puts them somewhere between parking attendants and debt collectors on the most hated jobs hot one hundred. Think of your campaign as reverse karma. By making what goes around come around for these pirates of our free time perhaps we can make the businesses realize that just because some shaved chimp with a phone book and an overfamiliar tone knows our first name, and insists on using it at the end of every sentence, we are not about to buy their stupid products.

Unless we were planning on getting new patio doors at an unbeatable, low, low price anyway, of course.

1) Wasting Their Time

Just like the rest of us, these bozos have schedules to keep to, targets to hit, and expenses to fiddle. So why not eat into their coffee-break time and mess up their manager's spreadsheets by taking up valuable minutes they could have been spending hassling some other poor sap with details on their latest incredible offers. The possibilities for doing this are as varied as the activities you might do in your own stupid job to waste a little time, but the impact here is of benefit to everyone, except your mark.

a) Insist that you are keen to speak to them and then put them on hold. Come back after 30 seconds and repeat that you are keen to speak to them (something the average telemarketer will hear about twice in his or her career) and put them on hold again. Repeat this until they finally give up.

b)   Go stupid on them. Listen to everything they say but whenever you get the chance ask them to go over things again. And again.

c)   Become foreign. Punctuate their pitches with frequent interjections. "Que?" is a good one. If they launch into fluent Spanish in an attempt to converse in what they take to be your native language, head north with a French "Pardon?" If all else fails just resort to a universal "Huh?" Say nothing else.

2)   Turning the Tables

These suggestions will waste their time too, but also require you to do a bit more of the talking, and therefore a little more work. However, as with most things in life, you only get out what you put in. A lesson that of course shouldn't be applied to anyone planning a bank robbery.

a)   Let your mark get through a healthy portion of their pitch, making appropriately encouraging noises where required. Tell the telemarketer that you're really interested in their product/service but you have to attend to a burning meal or unruly child right now. Ask for their home phone number and ask if it would be OK if you gave them a call to chat through your options later. Prolong your mark's squirming for as long as possible or simply launch headlong into a full blown tirade about why he/she thinks it is OK for them to call you at home but not for you to return the favour.

b)   As above, allow your mark to get through a good two thirds of their pitch and then take the opportunity to pitch them something of your own. It really doesn't matter what it is, though if you deal in timeshares, life insurance, or other investments it's a great chance for you to combine work with pleasure. Otherwise just use the airtime to promote your local church's upcoming autumn festival celebrations, or sing the praises of your neighbourhood dry cleaner. Refuse to sign up to anything unless they agree to a face-to-face meeting to discuss a joint business plan.

c) Take a padded cell approach to your dealings with any and all telemarketers. Many companies invest heavily in extensive training for their staff, teaching them how to get the best response out of their potential customers and recognise and deal with conflict before it happens. Use each call as an excuse to get rid of pent-up aggression (without lapsing into profanity) and see how much of your angst the keypad jockeys at the other end of the line are prepared to soak up before they end the call themselves. Keep in mind the holy grail of dealing with unsolicited phone calls that all revengers constantly strive toward—making the telemarketer cry.

3) **Weirding Them Out**

For those of you who would feel bad about being deliberately abusive to another human being (and who still consider these violators of the telecommunications infrastructure to be descendants of the same gene pool), there follow a number of suggested ways of getting your own back without resorting the kind of hairdryer bully boy tactics usually reserved for use by football coaches and stage-school parents.

a) Listen with animated interest to everything that your mark has to say. Ask them to go into elaborate details and take it all on board, rhapsodising about how wonderful what they are selling sounds, and how you believe that their product could indeed change your life. As they attempt to close the deal, tell them that you are happy to proceed and hand over your bank account details on one condition. That they will be your friend.

Explain that you had a friend once but they went away. At least you think they went away. They certainly stopped returning your calls. And answering their door to you.

b) Be an answering machine. Make your message suitably bizarre. If they attempt to leave a message, beep throughout it at random intervals. Once they have left a message, thank them for their time, but assure them that the homeowner has far too much good taste/sense to be interested in such a dumb product. If they attempt to engage you in conversation repeat that this is a recorded message and assure them that anyone who would try to engage in a chat with an answering machine is surely too dumb even to have a job in any industry, even telemarketing.

c) Assure them that the person they want to speak to is dead. Accept their platitudes before telling them that the homeowner hung himself with their telephone cord because they were forever being pestered by nuisance calls. Start to moan at this point with uncontrollable grief before hanging up.

d)   Talk through specific reasons as to why you can't possibly be interested in their products. So, if they're a cleaning company and they're trying to persuade you to have your carpets shampooed, tell them you don't have carpets. When they offer you discount rates on furniture polish as an alternative, tell them that termites ate all of your furniture. When they inform you that they offer an excellent pest-control service, ask then what the hell you are supposed to do if they get rid of your only source of food.

e)   Play paranoid. Demand to know where they got your number from. Jump to the conclusion that it was actually your partner that they were trying to get in touch with. Accuse them of trying to break up your marriage.

Face-to-Face With Doorstep Invaders

Nobody likes being disturbed at home. But those poor souls who ply their trade door-to-door are just doing their jobs, and good manners after all cost nothing. So if you're not interested in whatever it is they're selling, all you need do is politely inform them of this and allow them to go about their business, right?

Wrong.

It's bad enough getting dragged out of the shower after a hard day to answer a phone call about improving the look of your home with UPVC double glazing, but answering the door to these retards is more than anyone should have to put up with. The saps that treat these doorstep invaders with any kind of courtesy are making life harder for the rest of us. The revenger will create an environment that will have these streetwalkers conferring notes on why they should steer clear of your residence at all costs.

    A lot of these will work just as well with the salesmen, but sadly our society has become very inclusive where making a sale is concerned so you'll have to go a long way to freak out someone working on commission. However, with the weirdest and these days most prevalent of kooky cults, the ones that try and convert you on the doorstep, you are guaranteed results.

1) Naked Truth

Most religions (even bog standard Christianity) are united in a belief that the universe was created by a single conscious entity and man made a part of that. So why not answer the door in all your natural glory, that is, stark naked.

2) Looking Out

If you have a glass panel in the door, a nearby window that allows you to see outside, or a video entry system, go to the door but don't answer it. Just stand there. They will inevitably attempt to push a leaflet through your letterbox or under the door. When this happens, push it back out.

3) Invisible Callers

Alternatively, if your dwelling doesn't allow you to see who's outside the door before you answer it, open the door and look straight through them. Take a step out and look up the street as if you're searching for the kids who rang your bell and then ran away.

4)   Following Satan

Get them talking and listen with interest. When they ask you if you might be interested in attending a meeting tell them that you're concerned that their beliefs may clash with the views of the Satanic Fellowship that you currently worship with.

If they wish to discuss the matter further, invite them along to your next meeting. Entice them further with the information that Brother Baal has promised a live animal sacrifice to the hosts of the Dark Angel Lucifer, and that Sister Jezebel will be making her special recipe punch.

5)   Lap It Up

Lap up everything they say and tell them that you are very interested in joining their chapter. When they ask if you currently attend any religious services tell them that you don't at the moment, but that you used to be a member of their church in a neighbouring city.

Tell them that you were asked to leave when you felt compelled to burn down the meeting hall because you heard Jehovah's voice in your head telling you to do so. Assure them that you will do anything to be allowed back in and beg them to tell you where and when their next meeting is.

Don't Make Me Wait

On the face of it, the service industy's sole raison d'etre is the happiness and satisfaction of others. The staff that fill positions in this ever-growing business sector have made a conscious decision to work in a field that requires of them a certain level of humility and discretion, not to mention an understanding of basic psychology. So why is it that so many of them have the social skills of a stamping water buffalo and the modest self-awareness of Hillary Clinton? Well, maybe it has something to do with:

1) The hours they work.
2) The pay they get.
3) The fact that they're serving a slob like you in the first place.

OK, three good reasons for feeling a little aggrieved. But still no excuse for giving you a twist of lemon in your Martini when you specifically asked for an olive. So how should the revenger best get his own back on the surly server that threatened to wreck his evening with backchat and B.O. stains in his armpits?

After extensive research behind enemy lines, I have come to the conclusion that the best revenge is none at all. The reason for this is that not only does the service industry carry, pound for pound, more individuals with a predisposition to be revengers themselves than any other, but they also have the means to mount monstrously effective campaigns even in the short time that you're with them. Let's stick with our example of the simple waiter. Get on the wrong side of your waiter, and he can:

1) Spit in your food.
2) Put any number of other bodily fluids (or solids) in your food.
3) Make you wait forever for your food. No bad thing admittedly, if he's done 1), 2), or 3) to it.
4) Make you look stupid in front of your date.
5) Chat up and go home with your date.
6) Worst of all, tell your other half about your date.
7) Spill red wine on your shirt.
8) Spill white wine on your crotch.
9) Spill black coffee on your head.
10) Give you a table by the toilet.
11) Give you a table a long way from the toilet.
12) Send you to the wrong toilet.
13) Phone the police and tell them you're about to drive under the influence of alcohol.
14) Phone the police and tell them that your briefcase seems to be ticking.
15) Overcharge you.
16) Clone your credit card.
17) Run their keys down your bodywork.
18) Slash your tires.
19) Tell the chef to overcook your vegetables.

Maybe 19) is a given anyway, it certainly seems to be the case everywhere I eat, but that still leaves eighteen ways that a waiter in a restaurant can get back at you for your patronising tone, annoying laugh, or appalling decision to have Chardonnay with your beef wellington. And that's without even having to think too hard about it. So what are your options for revenge?

1)   Talk to the Manager

One option open to the dissatisfied diner is to ask to speak to the manager. If you need to express your contempt for the service you've received then by all means do so. But only once you've got the coffee. Otherwise the coffee bean will play only a supporting role in the beverage put in front of you.

The key to getting back at your waiter, or potentially even getting yourself a free meal, is not to worry too much about the reality of what actually passed between you and your server. The customer may always be right, but chances are that once you actually get down to what got your goat, it won't sound all that terrible. "He looked at me in a funny way" or "I had to ask for black pepper twice" are hardly grounds for dismissal. So get creative, and where possible implicate breaches of the restaurant health and safety laws. Try "He opened our Perrier with his teeth" or "He picked his nose while we ordered starters and flipped me the bird with the same finger when I pulled him up on it." Don't think of it as lying so much as embellishing an already subjective interpretation of your waiter's inherent attitude problem.

2)   How Was Your Dining Experience?

Should you find yourself in a somewhat lower class of establishment, you may be tempted to record your thoughts on one of the handy customer comment boxes. Do so by all means, but don't kid yourself for a second that these accusatory post-its, first made popular during the Salem witch trials, are transported directly to the manager by armed security guard. They're opened and read out by the staff like a theatre cast picking through bad first night reviews. Bearing this in mind, indulge your need to engage in damning written feedback only when you're eating outside your own neighbourhood. And adhere to the revenger's rule of not leaving any personal details. Pay by cash or expect nasty things in the mail, such as your credit card statement.

3)   You Can't Beat Them

The relationship between you and your waiter, like any between a master and servant, is a delicate and complex one. Most of us don't get the chance to be served very often so going out for a meal is our one opportunity to lord it up a bit. This is where we go wrong. Those that are used to the experience know that the real power lies not with the lord but with the serf, since it is the seemingly lower of the two that controls the other's environment.

A good waiter, by being aware of your needs, helpful without being pushy, and friendly without being smarmy, will make an evening. But by the same token a bad one can ruin it in a variety of ways. For this reason a revenger should approach a vendetta with those in seemingly menial positions with the utmost of caution. And for those new to the business of revenge, I can think of no finer training ground than to take a job waiting tables. You will learn all there is to learn about the noble arts of humiliation, deception, and messing with people's food, in a few short weeks.

Revenge in Art and Literature

Let's take a break from our training and consider some of the most infamous revenges to be found in the world of art and literature. Revenge has always been a popular topic for artists working in every form. Perhaps this has something to do with the fact that it almost always guarantees an audience the chance to vicariously experience those two staples of any entertainment, sex (usually the inciting incident) and violence (usually in the retribution meted out). Chuck in an MOR rock soundtrack and a cameo performance by Samuel L. Jackson and you've got just about any Hollywood movie of the last five years. But leaving that to one side—and let's face it, how many of us wish we had left The Long Kiss Goodnight and XXX to one side in Blockbuster Video—what do the great revengers of history have to teach us?

Hamlet, from Hamlet by William Shakespeare

Scenario:

 The original surly teenager, Hamlet emerges from a two-month sulk in his room to discover that his greasy uncle murdered his father in order to bed his mother and usurp his crown. As if that weren't enough for such a highly-strung young individual to take on board, Hamlet learns all this from the ghost of his dead father, now consigned to an airport lounge existence in purgatory between heaven and hell until the crime of his murder is put right.

Method:

 Hamlet affects an antic disposition (plays ga-ga) to buy himself some time and check out the ghost's story, before embarking on his revenge. Under a cover of borderline insanity, he turns several third parties—a troupe of traveling players, and his childhood friends Rosencrantz and Guildenstern, who his Uncle sends to spy on him—into weapons to be used against the king.

Outcome:

 Hamlet succeeds in ending the reign (and life) of his murderous uncle, with a poisoned blade that had been engineered to be the tool of his own death.

Overall Success:

 Hamlet ensures the king dies in a way befitting his original offence, that is with poison. But he farts around for so long writing bad lyrics for his student band and moping about his ex-girlfriend that by the time he gets round to it, not only has said ex drowned herself, but he's also been directly responsible for the deaths of five other people, including his own mother, and is about 60 seconds away from his own demise.

Final Rating: 4/10

 Some promising, if occasionally somewhat heavy-handed, groundwork with the players is let down by a shoddy lack of focus after the half-time interval, when Hamlet loses both the initiative and any sense of focus, regressing into hard-done by teen mode, and hitting out at whoever crosses his path rather than concentrating on the source of his woes. As a result, the only surviving major character is a drippy bookworm whose lament to our dead hero is quickly cut off by a jumped-up bonehead who arrives to try and figure out why it is the Danish Court suddenly looks like the last five minutes of a Tarantino movie.

Medea, by Euripides/Seneca

Scenario:

Having saved Jason and his backing group the Argonauts from certain death at the hands of her own father, Medea returns to Corinth as his wife, where her new in-laws make her feel about as welcome in their home as an outbreak of the ebola virus. No sooner has she borne her husband a couple of kids than it is suggested that for her own good she might want to quit the kingdom so that her spineless hubby can get hitched again to a new bride with considerably less baggage.

Method:

A background in witchcraft and sorcery is always a useful skill-set to be carrying into any revenge campaign, and once she's gently lured her hosts into believing she's down with the whole idea of relocating, Medea uses her talents to full effect, first by knocking together some bridal wear that's cursed especially for Jason's fiancée and then putting in place a plan for her own children that will ensure her name is put firmly at the top of the social services register all-time most wanted list.

Outcome:

Jason's new bride makes the fashion statement of the century in a stunning wedding gown that neatly changes colour in time for her own funeral minutes later. Having assured everyone that she's done with her tricks and that everything was down to a mix-up with the chemicals they'd used at the dry cleaners, Medea then murders her own children rather than leave them in the care of her understandably miffed hubby.

Overall Success:

 Medea does occasionally have a tendency to churn out speeches that sound like outtakes from a Courtney Love album. But unlike Hamlet, she knows when to get proactive, and when she strikes she does so decisively. Perhaps most notable of all is the fact that those she seeks revenge from are all left alive at the end of her campaign to contemplate the impact of her actions. Medea uses physical violence on relatively innocent parties to eke out emotional violence on her enemies.

Final Rating: 7.5/10

 The original Scary Spice, Medea takes the notion of girl power to a whole new level. As the lyrics might have gone: "If you wanna be my lover. You betta not betray me or I'll kill her and the kids too, zigga-zig-ah!" Truly, hell hath no fury quite like a woman scorned. However, Medea does not so much cut off her nose to spite her face as cut off her head to spite her little toe. The impact of her campaign is not in question; what might be is whether or not Medea is better off as a result of it.

Various Revengers from Jacobean Drama, by Middleton, Tourner, Marlowe, et al

Scenario:

Just as the success of Lock, Stock, and Two Smoking Barrels inspired a slew of imitative and frequently inferior mockney crime caper movies (including one particularly blatant rip off by Guy Ritchie of his own film), so the success of Shakespeare's most gruesome works, which were frequently rip-offs, sorry, I mean adaptations of other earlier works, led to the rise of the Jacobean tragedy with audiences in the mid 1600s. Jacobean tragedies were frequently driven by a revenge plot, and equally characterized by a hero who would become so coloured by the events of the play that it became increasingly difficult to actually work out who the hell the bad guy was.

Method:

Act I introduces us to our hero with a just cause for retribution, Act II–III shows his first attempts are met with contempt and often further infraction from his nemesis, dragging more victims and villains into the action giving our revenger further cause for retribution in Act IV, until things reach their bloody conclusion in an Act V leaving the stage resembling a Viking abattoir.

Outcome:

💀 The revenger always, but always, gets his man. Even if he dies or is horribly disfigured and/or brutally tortured in the process.

Overall Success:

💀 If Hamlet is drawn to the idea of revenge with a degree of reluctance and/or caution, then later characters, among them Shakespeare's Titus Andronicus, and certainly the revengers of Jacobean drama, seem to take too great a degree of relish in their campaigns. In *The Revenger's Tragedy*, the appropriately named Vindice becomes so enamored of his role of violent avenger that by the third act he has almost entirely sidelined his plot against Lussurio and is taking on the Duke, the Duke's sons, and indeed anyone else who seems to be of minor inconvenience.

Final Rating: 6/10

💀 Never afraid to get his hands dirty and embracing the revenger's lifestyle counts for a lot in the case of the Jacobean revenger. However, he loses marks for an over-reliance on the kind of gruesome violence which has brought the concept of revenge into disrepute ever since.

Zeus, from Greek Mythology

Scenario:

From the rich and varied history of the Mediterranean Sea come tales of incest, blackmail, empire building, and limitless wealth and power concentrated in the hands of a few twisted individuals. But enough about the royal family of Monaco, the ancient Greek Gods fought bitterly with their extended families, entertained themselves with meddling in the lives of mere mortals, indulged themselves, and punished those hangers-on they saw as deceitful to an extent that even Princess Caroline can only dream of. And above them all stood the J.R. Ewing of Mount Olympus, uber-god Zeus, always on the look out for a mortal getting ideas above their station to exercise his immense powers on.

Method:

Responsible in his time for suspending his own wife in chains from the sky with a manacle fastened to each limb, and for ensuring that disease and evil would be widespread once Pandora's box was open, perhaps Zeus's most famous revenge was against Prometheus, Titan friend to mankind. After the equivalent of slipping foreign currency into Zeus's collection box and then helping himself to a light from the barbecue in the back yard of Olympus, Zeus had Prometheus chained to a mountain peak and daily sent an eagle to tear out his liver, which would then grow back in time for the next day's feed.

Outcome:

 While Zeus had the satisfaction of knowing what Prometheus was up to, not to mention the fact that he now had a cheap and everlasting supply of bird food, Zeus's revenge had no impact on the race of man, which continued to be as insolent, offensive, and demanding in the face of punishment as a teenager grounded for the weekend.

Overall Success:

 Zeus was not someone to be messed with. He demanded tributes and showed he was willing to make an example of anyone, mortal, demi-god, or otherwise, who stepped out of line. And in choosing his punishment for Prometheus he ensured that even immortality was no defence against an effective revenge.

Final Rating: 6.5/10

 Like every other royal family since, the gods on Mount Olympus were themselves cursed with a surfeit of time, with little to worry about and less to justify their existence. Add this to the fact that golf would not be invented for several thousand millennia and it is easy to see how elaborate revenge campaigns could become a leisure activity to fill the time that ordinary mortals spent working just to put a roof over their heads. Zeus's campaign against Prometheus was forgotten after a mere few countless eons when Heracles, pre-sumably an ancestor of the English royal family, mistakenly shot the eagle, thinking it was the first grouse of the season.

Juliette de Merteuil from Les Liasons Dangereuses by Choderlos de Laclos/Christopher Hampton

Scenario:

 Eighteenth-century France was a pretty cool place to be, at least until the arrival of the world's first automated hairdressing machine. This is a rude awakening for those readers young and naïve enough to believe that contraception, divorce, recreational sex, and men's cosmetics were invented sometime in the latter half of the twentieth century. The baroque French society presented here is one where getting screwed is both the number one leisure activity and an occupational hazard for the aristocracy.

Method:

 When Mme. de Merteuil's estranged husband gets set to take a virtuous new young wife, Cecile de Volanges, Mme. Meurteil decides to arrange a series of special hen nights for her, enlisting the help of her sometime squeeze the Vicomte de Valmont.

Outcome:

 Not content with the level of challenge presented to him, Valmont extends the proposed campaign to encompass the seduction of a god-fearing, devoted wife Mme. de Tourvel, in return for the promise of one last night in the bed of his fellow plotter. While he is initially successful, he becomes unstuck as events escalate out of his control.

Overall Success:

 Mixed. A clinical revenge against her former husband is sullied by Mme. de Merteuil's encouragement of Valmont in his self indulgent and gratuitous campaigning. One gets the impression that we are in the presence of two former greats in the world of revenging who, while they still have a lot of the moves that made them famous in their repertoire, have got sloppy and careless with age.

Final Rating: 5.5/10

Merteuil and Valmont have been revenging for so long that they have forgotten what it is that drives a good campaign. And they are arrogant enough to believe that their undoubted skills will protect them despite the fact that by becoming emotionally caught up in the campaign (and by trusting one another with their secrets) they break two of the most fundamental rules of successful revenging.

Edmond Dantes from The Count of Monte Cristo, by
Alexandre Dumas

Scenario:

 An earnest and trusting young sailor, Edmond Dantes is implicated
in a loyalist plot to return the exiled emperor Napoleon to power
and unjustly imprisoned by those seeking to protect their own interests. As if to make matters worse, this all takes place on the night of
his wedding, leaving it too late for his bride to be to cancel their
Club Med honeymoon reservations.

Method:

 During his lengthy incarceration, Edmond completes his education
and within months of leaving prison is again a respected member of
the community, proving that outreach education programs in penal
institutions have gone downhill a little in the last two centuries.
During his thirteen years inside he is driven by the promise of
revenge over those that wronged him, and the hope that the newly
formed republic will get it's act together and introduce a parole
board system.

Outcome:

 Having secured fabulous wealth, his own title, a devoted manser-
vant and his own make of cigars, Edmond sets about dishing up
just desserts on the men that stitched him up under his new alias.

Overall Success:

Dumas, like Dickens, was a popular sitcom writer of his day, feeding a public hungry for more exploits of their favourite characters, a regular episodic dose in the newspapers and journals of the day. This may have something to do with the fact that while Edmond achieves all his major objectives and mounts an admirable campaign, he perhaps takes one of the central rules of revenging a little too far, biding his time for 117 wordy chapters.

Final Rating: 6.5/10

For a character that suffers so much at the hands of his enemies, Edmond takes relatively little pleasure in his campaign. While his style is admirable, it's hard to believe that his heart is truly in revenging. However just your cause, remember that it's important to have fun while you're wrecking the lives of those that have dared to cross you.

Iago from Othello, by William Shakespeare

Scenario:

 The Bard's second appearance in the top ten, and controversially not Titus Andronicus which features a notable recipe from the revenger's cookbook that may be of use to anyone with an oven large enough to bake a pie containing the two grown children of your mark. However, Iago shades it for sheer sneakiness, plotting revenge against his Moorish superior in the Italian navy, Othello, when he is overlooked for promotion.

Method:

With clever positioning and despite the fact that he bears a deep hatred for Othello, Iago is able to work his way into the Moor's counsel and torment him with insinuations regarding the virtue of his new bride Desdemona.

Unlike Medea, Iago does not have at his disposal an array of conjuring tricks or a propensity for violence. However, he proves himself to be highly resourceful in using whatever is at his disposal to achieve his aims: a disappointed former suitor of his mark's new wife, a handkerchief belonging to her, a charismatic lieutenant stationed with them in Cyprus, and his own talent for leading the mental paths of his victim's minds toward all the (wrong) conclusions, based on his own seemingly innocuous observations.

Outcome:

 Driven to the edge of madness by a jealousy that is entirely unwarranted, Othello smothers Desdemona, an act that prompts Iago's wife Emilia to badmouth her husband and reveal something more about his deceptive nature, leading to his capture and arrest.

Overall Success:

After mounting a hugely successful campaign, Iago throws it all away in the last few minutes. While he has undoubtedly wrecked his mark's career—not to mention marriage—he ends the play in bonds, refusing to speak, with the promise of the best that a seventeenth-century Italian torture chamber has to offer heading his way before his virtually assured execution.

Final Rating: 9/10

So much of what Iago does is textbook revenging that the real tragedy of Othello is the fact that the true hero of the piece didn't just hightail it at the end of Act IV. Cyprus is after all renowned for its excellent transport links, with Western Europe, the Middle East, and North Africa all a short jaunt away.

The Prince by Niccolo Machiavelli

Scenario:

Niccolo Machiavelli was born in 1469 in Florence, Italy. He spent his working life in the pay of the Republic, working as a statesman, political scientist, and diplomat, until a regime change in 1513 forced him into exile, where he began his life as writer.

Method:

Widely regarded as one of the basic texts of Western political science, The Prince is a practical treatise on governing and was presented to Lorenzo The Magnificent Di Medici by Machiavelli in order to help him stay in power. Written in a time of large-scale blackmail, violence, and conflict in a country that was beset by internal division and repeatedly won and controlled by foreigners, the book was notable for its amoral tone, citing examples of best practice as it did by such luminaries as Caesar Borgia, a butcher even in the eyes of sixteenth-century society.

Outcome:

After slogging his guts out in a succession of civil service jobs and getting his hands dirty during some notable military expeditions, Machiavelli was accused of conspiring in the downfall of Gonfaloniere Soderini. He was arrested, tortured, and imprisoned for this, though he maintained throughout that he was innocent. On his release he was forced to retire from public life and banished to his country estate at San Casciano, where he wrote The Prince. Since Oprah was still about 487 years away from plugging her first book on daytime TV, The Prince struggling from bad word-of-mouth reviews was not published until after his death, at which point it was immediately banned by the Pope.

Overall Success:

☠ Today, few people could name the Pope responsible for banning The Prince, or would ever have heard of the Medici that it was written for. But Machiavelli's name has become synonymous with intrigue, cynicism, and all the other qualities a revenger holds dear.

Final Rating: 9.5/10

☠ By all accounts a god-fearing and highly moral man, Machiavelli recognized that revenge far from being evil, was an essential and in many ways admirable part of human nature, and truly wrote the original handbook on it. The Prince should be required reading for anyone yet to dip into its pleasures, and while Machiavelli's long-term revenge campaign against the rest of the world on behalf of his beloved state was not to bear fruit for another 300 years after his death, Italy is now a united country, albeit one that changes governments like Jennifer Lopez changes engagement rings.

Judah Ben Hur from Ben Hur: A Tale of the Christ by Lewis Wallace

Scenario:

 In an epic plot that would today have Alexandre Dumas calling his lawyer for breach of copyright, Jewish prince Judah Ben Hur is betrayed by boyhood Roman friend Messala and sent into slavery.

Method:

 Judah befriends an older, wiser man on a no-frills package cruise, who later helps him out of captivity and finally puts him in a position to avenge himself.

Outcome:

 In a climax that was available only to Judeans of the time as a pay-per-view event, Judah and Messala are finally reunited in a grudge match chariot race.

Overall Success:

 Messala's Dick Dastardly attempts to fix the race are unsuccessful and Judah achieves minor celebrity, the release of his family, and paid holidays for all galley slaves and gladiators.

Final Rating: 8/10

 Forget the chariot race, the eleven Oscars, and that despite a ponderous three and a half hour running time, Jesus Christ warrants only

a brief cameo in a film whose title bears his name. The real revenge story of Ben Hur is Gore Vidal's script work. Despite Charlton Heston's best efforts to have Vidal—and the homoerotic subtext he brought to the relationship between Judah and Messala—removed from the picture, Ben Hur remains a classic and the ultimate gay love story gone bad. Vidal's classy revenge has stood the test of time far better than Heston's conservative jaw clenching.

Paul Kersey from Death Wish, by Brian Garfield

Scenario:

A liberal architect's world is shattered when his wife and daughter are attacked in their New York apartment. His wife is killed and daughter left in a coma.

Method:

After a business trip to Arizona, Kersey returns to New York tooled up and ready to take on any mugger that wants a piece of him.

Outcome:

After a few tentative steps into the wonderful world of vigilanteism, Kersey becomes bolder and is soon spouting one-liners as he dispenses with his hapless street-scum victims. He later goes on to stand for public office on a "zero tolerance" platform.

Overall Success:

☠ The Internet Movie Database cites a gross figure of $22 million for the first Death Wish, which spawned four, yes, four sequels and furthered the movie directing career of Michael Winner—Hollywood's own revenge on the movie-going public for indulging their appetites for senseless and graphic violence.

Final Rating: 1.5/10

☠ Paul Kersey and the world of Death Wish have sadly set the tone for popular revenging in the modern world. While the original movie showed some flair in its depiction of a man struggling with his conscience as he embarks on his first campaign, the sequels—and the structure of those many films they have inspired since—is entirely reliant on brutal violence, both in the original offence and in the payback achieved. Lorena Bobbit learnt all she knows about revenge from watching movies like this. Remember that violence breeds violence, and the more physical pain and suffering there is in your campaign, the greater the chance that some of it will be directed your way. Squeamishness may not be a quality that you should aspire to as a revenger, but be careful not to confuse squeamishness with a healthy distaste for the thought of your own blood being spilt, which is a both admirable and eminently sensible attitude to be taking into your campaign.

Keeping it in the Family

What Makes a Family?

 Families come in all shapes and sizes these days. Some don't have a Daddy. Some have two Mummies. Some have two Daddies and a Mummy. But enough about my building. What defines a family are the bonds that join it together. When everyone else has had enough of you, your family, in theory at least, should always be there to support you. This presents the revenger with a specific set of challenges when it comes to choosing elements of any campaign. Unless the aim is to critically rupture those familial ties, the revenger has to be subtle in his execution, particularly younger revengers who still have the misfortune of living with their parental units and older revengers whose offspring simply won't take the hints about "spreading their wings" and getting a place of their own, no matter how many times you try and change the locks.

The close quarter campaign depends on the revenger mastering a guerrilla mentality. Patience and persistence are the keys to modifying the behaviour of those around you until it is at what you feel to be an acceptable level. And if that all seems like way too much effort and you feel happy to let things roll along as they are, then there's every chance that your behaviour is already being modified by a splinter cell within your own unit. As always, trust no one, not even those you tuck in at night.

What follows are a series of suggestions for your campaign against those people who are always guaranteed a mention in everybody's list of what's most important to them, despite the fact that once you've left home you consider it a chore even to have dinner with them twice a year.

Dad

We'll start with the basics—and let's face it, there is no easier mark in the world to mount a campaign against than dear old Dad. By the mid-thirties, the human male father is a mess both mentally and physically. His dreams of life as a rock star or formula one racing driver long since abandoned, and deprived of his natural sleep patterns for as long as he has had children, Dad drifts through life in a semi-conscious daze, chauffeuring his children places as his mind contemplates his expanding waistline, receding hairline, and dwindling sex drive. The only negative thing to say about conducting a campaign against your Dad is that it'll prove to be about as challenging as outwitting a rocking horse. Beginners start here.

1) Losing Control

Since Mum now not only earns more than Dad, but also drives a car that looks like it should belong to a lumberjack when she does the school run, Dad has very few areas of prowess that he can feel secure in. But one of these is undoubtedly his wielding of the TV remote control. Undermine his sense of all being well in the universe by concealing it in the last places he would think of looking when he goes to the fridge for a beer. Stuff it in a magazine rack, behind a bookshelf. Every now and then move it just a few inches, under a cushion say, so that when he really kicks off about who's moved it it's still within his grasp. He will soon think that he's going mad, and with any luck Mum will too and dump him for someone with a bigger house.

2)   `Daddy's little Helper`

Dads like to make a big deal about the various projects they take on around the home, and fair enough too. I mean, where would your home be without that neat foot scraper by the back door that started life believing it was going to be an ornamental spice rack for Mum? Dad's weekend is filled with endless toil that he engages in with the sole aim of making the family home that bit more homely, right?

Wrong. Dad knows that if he didn't make himself busy then someone else would. Replastering the guest room may not be anyone's idea of fun, but it sure as hell beats an afternoon in the supermarket or the hell that is IKEA on the weekend.

So next time Dad starts moaning about how you never do anything around the house, tell him that you've made no plans for the weekend just so you could spend the time helping him out. Watch him squirm his way through Saturday as you tell him there's no need to go to the hardware store because you've just found a can full of the rawl plugs he said he needed. Ask him why it is that everything takes so long, and couldn't the two of you be doing something else why the window frames dry? Finally, suggest that it might not be such a good idea for him to be drinking beer while operating power tools. Don't be too surprised if at the end of the day he thanks you for your help and then gives you money to do something on your own on Sunday.

Alternatively, if it turns out that Dad really does work his butt off then just be as useless as you possibly can until he gives you your marching orders. If all else fails, injure yourself with a claw hammer. If that fails, injure him with a claw hammer. Make a note of the interesting new words you learn so that you can ask your teacher what they mean on Monday morning. Whichever of you ends up injured you should be safe from being asked to help out again.

3) **Hair Today, Gone Tomorrow**

Collect hair wherever you go that matches as close to your Dad's shade as possible. If you can, collect it directly from him—from his pillow, his spot on the sofa, or take to following him to the barbers. Once you've got a couple of dozen strands, you've got enough to put the frighteners on him whenever you want. Leave his hair somewhere he's sure to find it; circling his comb in the bathroom, say. Stick around and wait for him to find it and watch him age before your very eyes. If he throws the evidence away, collect it up for use again in a couple of days.

Mum

In contrast to the male, the female of the species, despite the physical rigors of a nine-month gestation period and the trauma of the birth itself, tends to come out of the child-rearing process with her faculties enhanced. Her hearing, in particular, becomes more acute, to the point that she can actually often hear a nappy being soiled from thirty yards through a dry stone nursery wall. While the lenses of her irises remain optically unchanged, the mother develops an intuition or foresight which allow her a degree of prescience that borders on the supernatural, allowing her to know that a vase is about to be knocked from the table or a domestic pet enraged by her offspring to the point of attack just before the event, allowing her to intervene in time. Added to the fact that unlike the male, who abandons all hope of fulfilling his dreams shortly after he is dragged to Mothercare for the first time, the birth of children gives the female an enhanced sense of how she may fulfill her own visions of a perfect life, if not for herself, then for her children at least. The fact that she is determined to provide these things for her children regardless of whether they want them, added to her improved mental and physical capabilities, make her a worthy adversary indeed.

1) All the Time in the World

Time is the one thing that the average mother, if there's such a thing, doesn't always have a great deal of at her disposal. Use this against her. When she's forced you to sit through a piano lesson "that she would've given her right arm for when she was your age," insist on teaching her everything that you learnt once the lesson is over. When she asks you if you've done your homework, tell her you're having trouble with your quadratic equations and ask for her help. Unlike fathers, mothers are genuinely hard on themselves about their own parental performance and she will be genuinely troubled by her inability to comprehend basic mathematical formulae and lack of interest in hearing you play chopsticks more than once. Once her eyes start to glaze over you'll know you're losing her, so say something like "It's OK, you don't have to play with me if you don't want to." At this point she will start laying into herself mentally for being such a lousy parent. And as long as she giving herself a hard time she'll lay off you for a bit.

2) Here's One I Made Earlier

A mother's Achilles' heel is unarguably her home. Strip away the layers of any Mum and you will find the never resting engine room of the obsessive-compulsive disorder that drives them. And let's face it, nothing untidies a lounge quicker than a whole bunch of people lounging around in it. So next time Mum wails at you for taking a room at its word and helping it to fulfill its role in life, take her at her word and get yourself a hobby. The messier the better. Action splatter paintings of the variety popularized by Jackson Pollock are guaranteed to involve you putting paint everywhere but on the canvas, and take up vast amounts of your mother's precious space. As an added bonus they require virtually no artistic ability to execute. If your Mum is one of those hippies that believes in free expression for her children, try daubing your work with swastikas.

3) He Followed Me Home, Can I Keep Him?

If your mother is so well balanced that she remains undisturbed by the twisted nature of your works of art, you're obviously going to have to work a little harder to send her into psychosis. Domestic animals will usually do the trick. Look at the Osbournes. Believe what you like about Ozzy's history of drug and alcohol abuse, it was trailing around his million dollar mansion after a herd of miniature pooches picking up dog poo that pushed him over the edge.

If your mother refuses to sanction even the notion of a pet in the house, get to work on Dad. Playing parents off against each other should be a crucial part in any campaign. After all, you've got plenty to get back at both of them for—they dragged you into this miserable world—so all it means is that you're killing two birds with one stone.

If neither parent approves of the idea then you're going to have to get to work making friends with the strays in the neighbourhood. Feed them, stroke them, and do anything necessary to get them to follow you home. Once they're in, you're home free. If your folks refuse to let darling little White Fang stay, accept their decision only through tears and tantrums until they either change their minds or bribe you out of your sulk with such an exorbitant display of treats and gifts you quickly forget about the stupid dog. If they decide to let him stay, agree that you will tidy up after him, feed him, etc. Stick to the terms for a week or so. Forget about them after that. Expect some stick from your parents, but shrug it off. They will quickly learn to take on the responsibility of looking after the poor dumb beast, and will be so weighed under by the extra work that they no longer have time to be checking on the state of your room.

4)   The Wrong Crowd

The great thing about Mum is that she's always willing to give you more ammunition. Mothers don't have time for debate about anything, so like the classic bad boss they not only claim to know what your problem is before you, they also have a pretty good idea of what the solution is to the problem you didn't even know you had. This can be intensely irritating but follow the revenger's code, take it on the chin with apparent acquiescence, and listen to her solution. The most effective revenges against Mummy dearest will always be those which seem to have come from her own suggestions. So the next time she starts bad mouthing your social circle, get yourself a whole new one. Come home extolling the virtues of your new best friend Slash. Tell Mum how you want to get a new tattoo just like his (or hers?). Ask if it's OK for you to go spend a weekend, and when Mum asks where your new buddy lives give her a seedy address on the wrong side of town. If you already live on the wrong side of town, give an address in the nearest deadbeat town that makes your neighbourhood look like a Swiss principality. Don't worry too much about whether or not these friends actually exist, although if you do want the added ring of authenticity there's no harm in bringing a few pierced deadbeats back home to meet Mum, as long as you're confident you'll be able to discourage them from ever repeating the visit. In most cases however, the idea that you're out with these people will be enough to make your mother go into furious overdrive and start asking you why you never see your old friends anymore.

5) Pay Your Way

Exactly the same principle, this time applied to the threat to chuck you out of the house unless you start paying your way a little bit. Balk at their suggestions of doing more around the house to help out and tell them that you will get yourself a job and start paying rent. Your options are now many and varied. If Mum prides your schoolwork above all else, tell her you've got a paper round and start leaving the house at 5am every morning. Fall asleep during dinner. If you rarely eat dinner with your family, or it goes unnoticed, start falling asleep during lessons at school and wait for the letters to start flying home. If social status is more of a concern for Mum, tell her you've got an after-school job in your local strip club/laundromat/ carwash. Tell her that your manager thinks you might have what it takes to work in the industry full time if you quit school now.

Brother

The pre-pubescent male spends most of his time playing video games in his darkened room avoiding attention from women and girls who find him cute. Then the magic of puberty kicks in and suddenly everything changes. From around the age of twelve he begins to spend most of his time playing video games in his darkened room avoiding contact with women and girls, all of whom he finds cute, but who now find him to be an unsociable acne-ridden slob, and rightly so. Brothers, like Dads, are relatively easy marks—sluggish due to sleeping late every day and mildly anaemic through lack of exposure to daylight, your greatest challenge in getting revenge on your brother may just be getting them out of their room for more than five minutes.

1) Whose Tape is This?

No matter how zealous your Dad is with labeling the family videotapes, you can bet that there are a few knocking around the house, usually tucked away in dusty drawers, with only a torn label on or a faded title of a movie no one in their right mind would ever want to watch: Star Wars Episode 1, for instance. Chances are that there are one or two knocking around in your brother's room. Under his bed, his mattress, concealed under a chest of drawers, even though he doesn't have a video recorder in his room. Dig these out when no one is around and pop them in the machine. Chances are they contain your bro's jerk-off material. Even late night repeats of E-Wild Palm Beach Spring Break Bikini Specials or lamely titled documentaries that are essentially edited softcore will do the trick. Now give them a nice new label and a title. Either "Mum's soaps" or something else you know she enjoys. Leave them lying on top of the family video and wait for the fireworks. There's always a chance that Mum will accuse Dad, but that'll just add to the fun, at least until your brother is confronted —his blushing will both confirm his guilt and give you a chance to top up your tan.

2) Exact Change Required

I was lucky enough to have a lock on my door when I was a boy. It only locked from the outside, and my parents kept the only key, but still I enjoyed the solitude that my attic room afforded me. Though lights and some furniture would have been a nice touch.

For most teenage boys, keeping everyone out of their room comes second only in their ongoing objectives to spending every god-given hour in it themselves. But despite the warning signs and accompanying threats that emblazon countless doors across the planet, the average child has to accept that their parents are allowed 24 hour a day access to them, at least until the decree absolute is served. So allow your brother the luxury of his very own bedroom door lock by feeding coins into the jamb while they're inside playing spot the musical evolution with their Limp Bizkit albums. Two or three slid in just above each hinge should do the trick, and for the connoisseur's touch you can hold them in place with a strip of tape. Needless to say, the real challenge here is finding a time when your brother was actually planning on leaving his room, so it's best perhaps used on an evening he'd planned to spend falling off his skateboard in the supermarket car park or when he's been left in charge. Just make sure that his door opens outward and that your parents are home before you let him out.

Sister

Taking on a sister, particularly a younger one, is a risky undertaking, due to the power and influence they wield in the average household. Consider the hierarchy of our "traditional" nuclear family, even if it's about as easy to find these days as coffee shop that doesn't require you to have a degree in Italian to order.

Family Hierarchy:

1) Youngest Girl

2) Youngest Boy

3) Mother

4)Father

Notice how age plays an important factor in determining the level of power exerted. There will be a subtle trade-off between sex and age and its effect on both our model children here, at least until they reach 13, at which point they will opt out of the system altogether and declare themselves independent of the parents before returning to their room to play skate metal on the stereos the parents recently bought for them. Sisters should be approached with caution, as they will hold a grudge for many years.

1) The Telephone

When your sister is out, pretend that a mystery male called for her. Pretend that his name is Josh and that he sounded very keen on her, but say that he left no other details. Girls have incredible imaginations and she will spend weeks, if not months, convinced that the love of their lives is out there somewhere, pining by the phone, wondering why she hasn't called back. Better still she might approach a real Josh at school and tell him she's sorry she didn't return his call but she must have lost his number, only to be met with a blank look and/or mockery for thinking that a hunk like Josh would be caught dead calling someone like her.

2) Railway Sleepers

This is a great way of putting the frighteners on a sister. Wait until she's asleep and creep into her room. Take your pillow along with two magilites, the brighter the better. Stand over her holding a torch in each hand and with your pillow between them. Now flick on the flashlights until you see her start to stir and then shout "LOOK OUT—TRAIN!!!" and drop the pillow into her face. If you can be bothered you might like to take a tape recorder or better still a camera in with you so you can capture her tormented screams for posterity.

Getting Even with the Government and Multinational Corporations

David and Goliath

 It would be easy to think that the multinational corporations and governments that make so many decisions on our behalf are in positions of such power that to seek revenge against them would be a shameful waste of a revenger's time and talents.

It would be easy to think this because it would also be right to. The art of revenging lies in mounting a campaign that stands a chance of success. Otherwise forget it. In this case, don't even think about it, unless you're already a president, prime minister, queen or king, or your name is a spoonerism of Gill Bates.

All Work and No Play

God's Revenge

 If you believe what they taught you in Sunday school, we brought the concept of work on ourselves when we ate an apple in the Garden of Eden and were subsequently kicked out and given an all eternity ban. Life in Eden had been cushy: plentiful fruit, temperate weather, and only the occasional (talking) serpent.

Since our untimely eviction, things have been a lot tougher for humanity: shame, guilt, physical frailty, and all the other things that make a good reality TV show were bestowed upon man, painful pregnancy on woman, and having to crawl around on its belly to the serpent, which poses the question of just how the talking snake was getting around beforehand. Anyway, wanting to give man a fighting chance in the world, God didn't take all the produce away, but he did ensure that the fruits of the world would from then on be new and improved with added extract of thorn and thistle. And so was born the concept of working for a living.

Cursed as we are with the existence of work, you might think that man might try making things easier for himself by entering into the spirit of joint enterprise with his colleagues, sharing the burdens borne by those weaker than he, and chipping in more than a foreign coin and piece of used tissue paper for Fred's leaving present. But sadly, the workplace is becoming the fastest growing arena for revenge campaigns. It was estimated last year that the western world lost more than 633,400,000 man-hours as a result of revenge-related absences from work. That's more than an entire month's worth of work lost by every Gemini albino working in the bowling shoe industry in Indonesia, in real terms. But how can putting someone into a position whereby they can justifiably take time off work be any kind of revenge? What follows are a series of suggestions for campaigns that will not only drive your mark to the edge of distraction, but also give them no grounds for legitimate time off work until such time as they make a deliberate effort to improve the working environment by handing in their notice.

Computer Blues

Computers are now the backbone of working life; if you don't use one at work yourself, there's every chance that you're paid by one, assessed by one, under surveillance by one, or set tasks by one. Either that or you just get paid to sweep round one.

The rise of the computer has led many analysts to imagine a Terminator-style future where the machines take over and hordes of homogenous cyborgs with Austrian accents scour the scorched earth in an attempt to eradicate all traces of humanity. Man has sought to stem this tide by imposing his own sense of individuality on the computer by using jazzy mouse mats. But the truth is that most of us are slaves to our machines and view them much as we do our children, as a source of occasional amusement and frequent heartache that seem to speak a different language to us and always seem to have a reason for not doing what's asked of them. If you're able to access your mark's machine, you can make his cyber life very difficult in a number of ways.

1) Who Turned off the Lights?

So simple yet so effective; turn the brightness down on your mark's monitor so that they are left with a black screen where next month's figures should be. Best used on the terminally stupid in a workplace where the IT staff take forever to arrive and are surly when they do, which is pretty much anywhere in my experience.

2) Parlez Vous Machine Code?

If you're using Windows, and let's not kid ourselves that anyone's using anything else, go to the start menu, click on control panel, and select regional settings. The control panel is the place to be if you're trying to get even with someone on their machine, and there are any number of things you can mess with, but this is the original and perhaps best. Click on the advanced tab and you'll get a page where you can choose the language settings for the machine. Choose one of the many variations on the Spanish tongue for a mark that you want to give a fighting chance to rectify the problem on their own. Choose Icelandic for a mark you really want to see suffer.

3) Shameful Screen Saver

This works best if you know your mark has an important meeting coming up where he'll be using his laptop to give a presentation. If you've got an image of your mark in a compromising position this is the perfect place to use it, but if not just find yourself a suitably depraved image from one of the many websites that cater to such tastes. Burn it onto a CD, and access appearance and themes on your mark's machine through the control panel as before. Now, add your image(s) to your mark's files; it doesn't matter where, as long as it has a folder of its own, and choose the slide show option for your mark's screen saver, selecting the file you've just created in the browse window as the source. Reduce the waiting time to five minutes so that your mark is just getting into the Questions and Answers session after their presentation before the slide show kicks in, or reduce it to two minutes if you want things to start happening before they've even made it to the end.

4)   Quick Decorating Job

Alternatively you could just use the same method to alter your mark's wallpaper so that they're greeted with the image of your choice the next time they turn on their screen. Open the image on their machine and right click on it, then select "set as desktop background" before you shut down.

5)   Hide and Seek

Best used when your mark is struggling to make a deadline. Find the files that they've been using most recently in the Documents Tab of the Start Menu and go to the folder that they're kept in. Right click on the folder and then select Properties. Tick the box at the bottom marked Hidden. Come out of the folder and go to the windows task bar at the top of the screen, and under the Tools options select Folder Options and then View. Check that it is set not to show hidden files and then clear your mark's recent documents in the advanced section of the control panel start menu. Watch your mark start to lose it when they can't find the file they were using just a minute ago and then you can either step in as a benevolent PC guru or just step out for an extended lunch break.

Getting Back at Your Boss

While you could indulge in any number of campaigns against your line manager, the sad fact of it is that there's every chance you will be the one that ends up sorting things out on their behalf. So the following suggestions are specifically designed to ensure that they won't stop you from leaving in time for your T'ai Chi class.

1) Job Description

We live in an age where our performance is monitored, tabulated, and evaluated, allowing our employers to give us up to the minute and statistically backed-up reasons why we can't have a raise this year either. But however bad you think you may have it in this department, your boss has it worse, having to deal with any number of responsibilities that are beyond your consideration, managing you being just one of them.

Take a little of the burden from your mark's executively strained shoulders by getting hold of a copy of their job description. This one works particularly well when your mark has been promoted ahead of you into a role you had your eye on, as there's every chance you'll already have a copy of the breakdown, but if not you should be able to get hold of a copy from personnel, or human resources, or whatever the department that deals with employing people is calling itself this week. Most job descriptions will not only list core responsibilities for the employee fulfilling the role, but also percentage figures outlining what proportion of their time. Dig out some of the more obscure responsibilities and ask for a team meeting on them. Seek further clarification on points that they are obviously unclear on. Make a note of how your boss seems to spend their time and how it tallies with what it is they're actually supposed to be doing.

2) Evidence

Make a note of anything even vaguely incriminating that your boss says and look for opportunities to use it. Make a note of the date, time, and location. Don't worry too much about the context of what's being said, as this will often lessen the impact, just record the "facts" of what was said. The great thing about written evidence is that it's very easy to take it the wrong way, so if you were to ask your boss which of the two competing projects they wanted you to focus on they might be happy to leave you to make that choice for yourself. But when you record the exchange in writing, it looks bad on your mark:

Mon 12/04/04, One on One meeting in CR2: Was given the response "Whatever" when I asked my boss whether he wanted me to focus on the Compliance documentation or the new ratings system this week.

Keep your evidence short and snappy, and don't be drawn into a long discussion about what happened. Stick by your evidence and don't deviate from it. It's a sad fact proven all too often in the media that people are far more willing to listen to a brief, damning headline than a complex, measured statement, even if it's the latter that is closer to the truth.

3) Stay Focused on the Negative

One consequence of following the above suggestions may actually be that your boss gets a lot better at their job, making sure that they focus on what they are actually employed to do and being tactful and considerate in their dealings with you. It's a galling thought that a mark might actually improve their life situation as a result of your attention, but one that every revenger has to face at some point in his career. At this point you have three options:

i) Abandon your campaign as your boss has now become relatively pleasant to work for.

ii) Tag along for the ride for the moment, since there's every chance that your mark's improved position will benefit you, but keep in mind the fact that a mark is a mark until you decide otherwise. Be ready to resume your campaign at a moment's notice.

iii) Keep up the pressure.

While a long-term campaign is to be applauded, let's focus on what to do if you're determined to make them pay short term. Deal with your manager as you hate to be dealt with yourself. Remain negative about their achievements and always focus on what you feel they could be doing better or more of. Say as little as possible in your dealings with them but give them no reason to question the quality of your work, while maintaining your evidence log. Ensure that you are only ever surly and uncommunicative with your mark and remain friendly and open with everyone else you work with. Managers tend to hate the thought of not knowing what's going on with their staff, and sooner or later they will confront you about it. Remain tight-lipped and wait to see what they are prepared to venture in order to open you up—it may be something about their attitude to the company, to their boss, or even their personal life, but it is bound to be something you can use against them. Managing your manager can feel like you're involved in a Mexican stand off that lasts for months as opposed to minutes, and as a result can be extremely hard work, but it always pays dividends eventually.

Levelheaded Revenge

For all the emphasis laid on teamwork, most managers can't bear the idea of their teams getting on with one another. A workplace where everyone is honest and open, respectful of each other's roles, willing to share information, and united by common objectives is, after all, an environment where managers are surplus to requirements. The revenger should therefore question his own motives before embarking on campaigns against his colleagues. Only when you are sure that your ends are selfish, petty, vindictive, and purely for your sole gratification should you indulge in any of the following:

1) **Missing Ink**

Aren't today's modern, paper-free offices great? Help your mark toward achieving every filing clerk's dream by removing the ink cartridge from their printer and hiding the replacements behind the coffee machine.

2) **Up Close and Personal**

Ask for a quiet word with your mark. Tell them that you have been nominated to speak to them by other members of the team who wish to remain anonymous. Tell them that they seem to have a personal hygiene issue, which may be acceptable in other environments, but due to the close working space you occupy here is starting to impact on the performances of other members of the team. Make sure you do this at the start of the day so that they have a few hours to stew in the shame.

3) Ghostly Messages

Remove any messages left for your mark while they're stuffing themselves on the buffet special at Pizza Shack. Make sure you're not spotted. Keep them for a few days and then put them back.

4) Online Gossip

Indulge in some juicy gossip with your mark. Encourage them to dish the dirt on subjects and individuals you know they have a particular passion for. When they send their reply, remove your original mail from the top and send your reply, which should be short and un-incriminating, to everyone on your mailing list "by accident."

5) Office Romance

Send your mark a short love letter from a web-based account. Tell them that you've been watching them for a while and think you'd like to get together with them. Ask them to meet you by the water cooler, or somewhere else in your sight line, and see what happens. Make your next e-mail an apology for not turning up, and explain that you're very nervous about meeting them, but would like to get to know them better. Make your demands for the next meeting more absurd or outrageous. Many marks will go along with your requests for weeks, persisting in the belief that their mystery office romancer is genuine. A great way of gathering information on your mark for an extended campaign.

6) Imaginary Phonecalls

The telephone is an extremely vital social tool in the workplace, especially for sales people on commission. They get very cranky when you don't give them their messages in the level of detail that captures every nuance of the caller's intention. So be sure to give your colleague all their messages as soon as they get back to their desk, including the bogus one you just made up. Tell them John from the purchasing deparment phoned.

Be unable to tell them anything about the call other than that he sounded really keen to talk to them about a business venture. Be prepared for an ear bashing for not recording his number or surname, though for added effect you could give them a local number and then apologise for getting a digit wrong when they are unable to find their mystery buyer at the other end of it.

7) Bonus Bike Locks

The horrors of commuting on public transport has proved too much for a lot of workers. Cycling is an essential way of keeping fit, whilst beating the traffic and is environmentally friendly to boot. It's also a great way to get revenge on an annoying colleague. People are incredibly precious about their bikes and hate to think of them being tampered with. It is your duty as a kind workmate to help protect your colleague's pride and joy.

Ensure that their bike is secure at all times by purchasing a lock of your very own to double up on their existing one the next time they cross you. Hide the key somewhere that they would never think of looking, such as under the pile of paperwork that has been growing in their desk for the last six months.

8) Do Your Job

It is not often that important to stress the value of following rules in a revenge campaign, but the best way to achieve revenge over those you work with is by achieving all that you can in your job and advancing until you're in a position to have direct and meaningful power over them. Bend the rules by all means, just make sure that you don't get caught doing it. And if you work in an organisation that doesn't recognise your undoubted talents, then it's probably time to move to one that does. This will leave you free to fulfil your life potential away from those that would conspire against you and plan an all-out, gloves-off campaign for the time it takes to serve your notice.

Sharing Your Abode

Maybe you're reading this swinging in a hammock in the jasmine garden of the villa on your private island in the Bahamas. In which case, congratulations on your good fortune and you have my permission to skip this chapter. Come to think of it, you can probably skip the whole book. You're more likely to be the target of someone's revenge than have an ax to grind of your own, and if you're still unhappy then there's probably nothing that I or anyone else can say to make you feel better, you rich crazy freak.

For the rest of us, co-habitation will at some point have formed an unavoidable part of the life experience. While there's no doubt that family and partners can be prime sources of irritation and therefore worthy targets of a campaign, the revenges suggested here are primarily aimed at those incidental invaders of our space. Their presence is merely temporary and therefore they can be targeted with more venom and less concern for long-term fall out than would be the case with those that share our DNA.

Having said that, there's nothing to stop you from adapting elements of these campaigns for use against your nearest and dearest. Just don't blame me when you end up on the Holidays from Hell edition of Jerry Springer for messing with the Christmas turkey.

Roommates, houseguests, neighbours, these are our intended targets. People that we all too often share a large proportion of our time and space with unintentionally, and who all too frequently fail to recognise the boundaries of tolerance.

The Revenge Seeker's Cookbook

One of the true horrors of flat sharing is that little piece of Palestine in your very own kitchen, the communal refrigerator. Long the source of interminable strife and countless unworkable resolutions, the following recipes for revenge are sure to make your mark think twice about helping himself to any of your food stuff ever again.

1) **Chili Cores and Seeds**

Adding Tabasco, Encona, or whole chili peppers to a dish is an obvious way of giving it an unexpected punch. Unfortunately it is all too easy to spot a whole chili and the strength of a ready made sauce will often unbalance the overall flavour of the dish, thus alerting your mark after a single mouthful. Adding the white, rind-like flesh from the inside of the chili, and/or the seeds, allows you to be extremely creative with your choice of dish without giving the game away, and still adding a fiery and distinctly unpleasant aftertaste. Works best in sweet dishes such as yogurts, trifle, and granola.

2) **Milk**

It's often the basics that other people run out of and think it will be O.K. to borrow a little of, even if you were saving that last bit for your morning coffee. And we all know that there are people who even though they've been shopping that day, will still choose to use your milk rather than their own. So the revenger should always make sure that the milk shelf is kept well stocked. Keep a spare carton in your bedroom for a fortnight or so under the bed, in a drawer. Anywhere it won't be seen and has no chance of staying cool. Then, transfer the contents into a fresh carton, tipping the fresh milk away first. If the carton you're using is clear you might want to break a few of the bigger lumps up so that your mark is unaware that the contents are clearly in the process of evolving into an animate life form. This works best on a Friday or Saturday night, or any night when your mark is likely to come in inebriated and swig straight from the carton. If you can, stick around and see if your mark actually manages to make it to the sink in time to get rid of their mouthful of viscous dairy gloop.

3) Soap

Soap comes in so many different forms these days (liquid, deodorising, anti-bacterial) and such a variety of colours, that you can really get creative in the kitchen with it. The key here is to be subtle. Most people, particularly the kind that steal other people's food, won't be put off by a faint soapy taste as they'll assume the plate they're eating from has not been dried properly and press on. So, a little goes a long way in any dish, and with the right dosage you can actually leave your mark unaware that they have been spiked, at least until they notice the aftertaste in the back of their throat as they pay a visit to the smallest room in the house for the third time that hour. Liquid soap tends to work best on deserts or mixed into stews and casseroles. Hard soap can be grated onto shepherd's pie, pasta, and pizza. Use a combination of bars in different shades for that authentic Quattro Formaggio effect.

4) Sweet Revenge on Sweet Tooths

In most cases, the revenge dish is best modified when it is in near liquid form, since sauces, stews, and so on are far easier to mix your surprise ingredient into. But the adventurous revenger can obtain spectacular results with just a little effort, either by investing in readymade pastry cases and cooking chocolate, or by simply bastardizing the originals. Take six miniature fruit pies and create your own selection pack by carefully removing the pastry lids and scooping out the contents, replacing the fruit with whatever takes your fancy, such as horseradish sauce, lard, and mustard. Something that you know for a fact your mark will find repulsive. And if chocolate is your guzzling roommate's preferred choice of stolen snack, then why not rustle him up some homemade cookies with cheap cooking chocolate and the best dog biscuits money can buy?

5)   **Labels**

Labeling food is a well-intentioned, if somewhat naive, attempt to remind refrigerator thieves that what they are doing is ultimately wrong. However, the revenger knows that such tactics are futile. Still, labels can be fun when you switch them around a little, prompting internecine strife within the household, which the revenger can observe from a safe distance. This works particularly well when there is more than one pantry burglar on the prowl. Or better still, come up with your own labels tailored according to your mark's tastes and take enormous pleasure in seeing a sanctimonious vegetarian wolf down a mouthful of Kung-Po chicken thinking it's bean curd.

Tidying up

It can be truly annoying when your roommates transgress the unspoken agreements about keeping the place tidy. However, the annoyance is usually dismissed as relatively insignificant when the idea of a cleaning rota is mooted. The successful revenger knows this and would be the last to suggest anything so lame. Far more effective than honestly and openly discussing the problem with his co-habitants and looking for possible mutually acceptable solutions, the revenger might try one or all of the following:

1)   **Secret Slug**

Yep, you guessed it, you're gonna have to sacrifice a slug for this one, so those of you averse to the idea of martyring a slimy common or garden invertebrate in the name of sweet revenge might want to look away now. Take your slug and place him in an empty 35mm film canister. Any container of similar size will do, but a film can is an ideal size, making this a perfect revenge to play on photographers, who in my experience have a total disregard for the order of anything other than their precious portfolios, but there you go. Anyway, take your live slug and imprison him in his plastic tomb. Now leave the canister somewhere it's not likely to be found for a while. By the vacuum cleaner, say. Or under your mark's mattress. Unfortunately it is in the hands of the gods to a certain extent who opens it, so you do have to choose your spot well. But whoever opens the canister and instinctively pokes their head toward the opening to see what's inside is in for a smell sensation unlike any they've ever experienced before.

2)   **Bathroom Bubbles**

Bit of an odd one this as the best time to use it is when your lazy roommate has actually done some cleaning, in the bathroom. Ideally used when they've got guests over, such as parents, someone they've just started dating, wealthy maiden aunts, anyone they might be keen to impress even slightly. Use the facilities yourself (as you won't have a chance to do so later), flush, and then once the tank has refilled empty a generous portion of washing-up liquid into it. A whole 500ml bottle, in fact, should do it. Now retreat and wait for the cries of despair from the next person to flush and be met with a tide of bubbles reminiscent of a bad fifties monster movie. It's important to be around for the inquest. Obviously your roommate will be absolutely delighted that you are on hand to offer your helpful thoughts on their inability to do something as simple as clean a toilet, and to agree with suggestions from their visiting guests that they are clearly a little out of practice as far as cleaning goes.

The Joy of Houseguests

Greater love hath no man than he that invites others into the bosom of his home to spend quality time. And greater irritation hath no man than when those guests, having spent the weekend taking of his hospitality, drinking his beer, hogging his couch, and taking complete charge of the remote control, decide to extend their visit in order to "miss the Sunday night traffic." Smile through your tears and try a couple of these strategies for reminding your houseguests just whose place it is.

1)   Marble Madness

You'll need young kids with old-fashioned tastes in toys for this one to be a success, as it doesn't work with Nintendo Game Cubes. Believe me, I've tried it. Firstly, clear some space in your bathroom cabinet, making sure to remove and store any items of value, such as expensive fragrances or diamond-studded nail scissors. Now slide a piece of thin card (the side of a cereal packet is perfect) so that it comes to rest on one of the shelves inside. Now start feeding the marbles into the cabinet and hold them in with the card. A couple of dozen should do it, but use as many as you feel like. Carefully shut the door and remove the card.

It is a scientific fact that the average houseguest cannot resist a quick peek at what's in the bathroom cabinet and we can only guess at what they're hoping to find. Either way, you'll know as soon as they do it. Needless to say, this works best on tiled floors.

2) Dodgy Socket

Clear nail varnish has become something of a staple item in any make-up kit these days, or so I'm told. It's also a useful tool to have in your revenger's kit. Paint some onto the prongs of an appliance that your houseguest has brought with them (hairdryer, electric razor, mobile phone charger) and the item in question will refuse to work. Make sure the varnish has time to dry before the item is used that is unless you want to damage the owner as well. This can also be an effective way of shutting down noisy roommate's sound systems, though getting them to stop singing might be a tougher prospect.

3) Just not Cricket

This is a real last resort, unless you've got an enormous house, in which case, who are you to complain about the odd houseguest? Anyway, crickets are non-venomous, difficult to track down, but extremely sociable creatures that like nothing better than to while the hours away having a good old jaw. Not that their primary form of communication involves their jaws, but rather the charming sound that occurs when the male of the species rubs its front wings together in search of a mate. I say charming, but after a few hours this noise will grate on even the hardiest of free-loaders, particularly since the cricket is primarily nocturnal.

Release a few of these into your guest room and they'll be packing their bags in no time. If your temporary lodgers claim to be unaffected by the interminable insect chatter simply move them into alternative accommodation, such as the garden shed, on the advice of the exterminators you haven't contacted for help. Crickets can be bought at any good sized pet store, who may also be able to help you out with a snake or large spider to get rid of them once your guests have actually taken the hint and cleared out.

4)   Rat Traps

As with a lot of the most effective revenges, this works on a purely psychological level. You didn't think I was going to suggest releasing live rats, did you? O.K., after the crickets maybe you did. But if you were to get enough big ones they might actually stand a fighting chance of taking down the spiders and snakes that have been terrorising your home since they grew fat on all the crickets. And they are a real pain to get rid of once the guests have been scared away.

A couple of rattraps can add the perfect finishing touch to any guest room. For maximum impact, make sure that they're displayed prominently in bare corners and empty cupboards, and make sure you tell your guests it really isn't anything for them to worry about since they probably won't see a rat for the duration of their stay. With the emphasis on the "probably."

What's Mine Is Yours

Living with a roommate can mean learning to compromise and share your personal living space. It can also involve funding a sponging layabout who sees you as another form of cash point. If you don't want this loser living off you forever, a lesson must be taught.

1)   Doggy Bag

If you're a little tired of being an alternative source of funding for a lazy roommate, why not invest in a cheap wallet or purse and take it out with you go for a walk? Go to the local park and find some of the local dogs' recent offerings. Place this offending item into the wallet and then leave it lying around in your flat somewhere that your roommate's jackdaw fingers are sure to find it.

Neighbours

 You can choose your friends, and with the proliferation of Web sites for adoption agencies and East-European mail-order brides you can now choose your family too. But for many of us, the neighbours are something that's forced on us.

Revenge Gardening

Some gardens are a disgrace to the community, and bring down the tone of the neighbourhood. Mine would be a perfect example of that. Forced to choose between hours of ceaseless toil with trowel and watering can and a few simple guerrilla operations carried out under the cover of darkness, the revenger can swiftly drag down neighbouring gardens to the level of their own picket-fenced wasteland in just a few minutes a day or night.

1) The Joy of Weed Killer

As always, the key is to be subtle in the use of industrial weedkillers. Make a note of which of your green-fingered neighbours plants have been neglected of late, and target these for special attention. Or select those that have been receiving love, attention, and meaningful conversation to promote the nagging thought in your mark's mind that they have been killed with kindness. Above all, do not take the nuclear approach and attempt to wipe out everything in one fell swoop as your mark will immediately suspect that something is up. Far better to operate an ongoing campaign, taking weeks off from time to time to allow you the pleasure of watching your mark run around desperately and thinking they've just got on top of things again before you launch another assault.

2) Lend a Helping Hand

The environmentally friendly revenger might like to consider using one of the many lawn supplements currently on the market to help his neighbour's lawn along. A prescribed dose of iron oxide, the major ingredient in most such products, will produce a green pigment in any lawn that a professional groundsman would be proud of. Double the dose and you'll have a lawn in a shade of black that would delight the Addams family. If you're pushed for time, or the lawn in question is particularly large, why not write a brief message for your neighbour with the solution? You may have to wait for a period of heavy rainfall for this to take effect, but as with all the best things in life, the anticipation is half the fun.

3) Vegetable Surprise

On a similar theme, why not add some unexpected crops to your neighbour's patch? The turnip seed is one of my favourites, as it is notoriously hardy and will resist all but the most determined efforts to curb its growth, and was last considered a delicacy centuries ago.

4) Sugar-Coating

The great thing about sugar solution is that it won't be noticed by your neighbour, as unlike chemical foods it leaves little trace. Indeed, in the short term, your mark's garden will seem to be thriving as sugar figures as an ingredient in most plant foods. However, it won't just be the plants that are enjoying your clandestine fertility treatments. Ants, wasps, beetles, and just about every conceivable bug that buzzes, crawls, or flies will soon be making a beeline for your mark's turf, which will quickly come to resemble an open audition for an Irwin Allen movie. And once word's got round, the bugs will bring the birds.

And so the glorious circle of life goes on, in a living, breathing, moving tableau, as your neighbour seeks to play his own part in nature's wondrous cycle, fending off angry wasps high on sugar and ravenous gulls trying to feast on the bloated ants that have taken over his lawn. Sugar solution, which you should make with about a kilo of sugar per five liters of water, need only be the start.

See how the squirrels make out when you spread peanut butter on the bark of your mark's trees and shrubs. My bet is that they'll be so busy gnawing on their nutty treat that they'll lose all track of where the Sunpat ends and the shrub begins. And if your mark tries to combat the insect invasion with insecticide, don't forget that birds are creatures of habit and come to depend on regular and fixed sources of nutrition, so you'd best supplement their diet with some birdseed on the flowerbeds.

Car Wars

If, like me, you live in a city, you'll appreciate the importance of having a car. At times it seems to me that without the car, the economy of a city would be in permanent recession; no more revenues for parking fines, and come to think of it no more work for the guys digging up the same roads day after day. However, this chapter is not directed at the politicians who are happy to tell us to take the bus as they step into their chauffeur-driven limos, but at that other scourge of the modern city motorist, the moron that just took our parking space.

1) Handle with Care

Leave a little honey on the underside's of your mark's door handle for their return. Usually there is nowhere to wash your hands and the honey may also attract wasps, ants, and other such delightful creatures to your mark's car.

2) Feed the Pigeons

If honey just isn't your style, a couple of slices of bread or some seed will allow you to get your own back. Spread the seed/scatter the bread in crumbs over the hood and roof of your mark's car, or over the interior if, joy of joys, they're driving a convertible. The urban pigeons will be on it in no time and make themselves totally at home and once they've had their fill they'll leave their own special tributes to their benevolent host.

3) Stop Scratching It

Keys down the paintwork? Very nineties. No real class. Superglue in the central locking? O.K., now we're talking. Make a statement.

4) Ping-Pong

You'll need access to the gas tank for this one. You'll also need some good quality table-tennis balls. Slip a half-dozen of them into the tank. This can work with just one, but hey, the more the merrier. What this will do is turn your mark's car into something that resembles an old fashioned bingo-caller's machine. After a couple of hundred yards the engine will be warmed up and the balls will get sucked up and block up the fuel line. The car will stall and the balls will float down into the tank again. The car will then be fine for another few hundred metres before it stalls again. This will last until your mark gives up and calls a mechanic.

5) Alternative Air Freshener

There's now a bewildering range of air-fresheners available to mask the smells of cigarette smoke, junk food lunches, and any unwashed children that might be lurking in your car. Now you can supply your mark with their very own tailor-made fragrance. Mix a solution and pour it into the gap between the bonnet and the windshield. This will heat up on the engine and get sucked in through the vents into the interior. You might like to try a mix that blends the delicate flavours of canned tuna fish residue, sour apple juice, a solution of past their sell by date prawns with rotten potato peelings, and perhaps gone-off soup for that truly personal touch.

6) Message on a Window

Glass etching spray is available from all good art shops and allows you to truly express your feelings to whoever has wronged you. Profanities are all too common in today's society to have any true impact, so try leaving a message that is a little more individual, and also likely to raise the eyebrows and even hackles of local-law enforcement officers such as "I DEAL DRUGS" or "STOLEN CAR."

7) Well-Oiled Window

For a less personal but equally irritating revenge, tear back the rubber insulation on a side window and tip oil into the gap beneath it. The thicker and gunkier the better. Now whenever the window is rolled down it will get covered in oil and your mark will actually have to take the door apart to rectify the problem.

8) Where's Rover?

This one will take a fair bit of work and is not for the squeamish. You're going to need a dog lead and a dead dog. Just so we're clear on this, I am not suggesting you go out and kill a dog. I mean, unless you were going to anyway. No, I am still joking, of course, but should you come across one, after of course you've done everything you can to find it's owners but to no avail, then you could use it in the name of revenge. Alternatively you could just go to the butcher's shop and buy a couple of kilos of offal and patch together a dead dog of your own.

Anyway, attach your dead dog to your lead and then attach the lead to your mark's rear bumper. You've now got two options. If you can't be bothered to play any further part in this stunt, just place your dead dog in front of his rear wheel, as if the poor beast had managed to keep up with him all the way from his house but then got caught out when your mark went into reverse to park.

Alternatively, if you consider yourself a capable actor, physically fit and capable of keeping a straight face, leave your dead dog behind the rear of your mark's car and await his return. Once your mark has got back in his car, wait for him to pull out, allow him to get near the car park exit, then run after him. Carry with you a Frisbee, tennis ball, or whistle any kind of dog walking paraphernalia. Scream and shout. If and when you reach your mark's car, thump on the side and get him to stop. Burst into tears and berate him through your sobs. Ask him what you're supposed to tell your daughter when she asks where Rover is?

Happy Now?

The Revenger's Lifestyle

 And so we reach the end of our guide to getting back at those who made the mistake of messing with someone who has chosen to dedicate their life to the pursuit of revenge. You now have every skill at your disposal to become the perfect revenger.

It is perfectly natural to feel a little empty at the end of a campaign, so don't be too surprised if you discover that humiliating, ruining, or otherwise dealing out justice to those that deserve it doesn't bring you quite the pleasure you had perhaps anticipated. The revenger knows that life is full of disappointment, and realises that it may be impossible to ever feel truly happy for more than an fleeting instant. However, he can raise his own level of contentment by making it his mission in life to ensure that those around him are consistently miserable and eke out their existences in a atmosphere of perpetual fear, never knowing where the hammer might fall next. Creating constant paranoia for those around you should be the ultimate goal.

Knowledge can be both a bountiful blessing and a terrible curse. As a revenger you must never forget that it if you must view every relationship you have with the utmost cynicism, as if you do not consider even the most seemingly innocent request or encounter with a deep and abiding suspicion that borders on the paranoid, then the chances are you could already be someone else's potential mark.

The Pre-Emptive Future of Campaigning

With this in mind I leave you to embark on what I hope will be a successful and vindictive career in revenge. I hope you find the suggestions in this book of some use, but if you take only one thing from this guide, it should be that knowledge is power.

Keep your eyes and ears open at all times around your friends, relatives, colleagues, and loved ones, and make notes if you need to. Record PIN numbers and bank details whenever you get the chance as it is this kind of information your potential marks will be most protective of should the time come when you have to take action against them. Keep yourself mentally sharp when you're not in the midst of campaigning by plotting means by which you use the fruits of your harvesting should they ever be so foolish as to cross you. Soon you'll realise that you are in such a position of power that the only thing stopping you from taking a full and fruitful revenge on those around you is the unfortunate fact that they have done nothing to deserve it.

But why let a little thing like that stop you?

Index